Interactive Acting

INTERACTIVE ACTING

Acting, Improvisation, and Interacting for Audience Participatory Theatre

Jeff Wirth

Fall Creek Press
Fall Creek, Oregon

Library of Congress Cataloging-in-Publication Data

Wirth, Jeff, 1957-
      Interactive acting : acting, improvisation, and interacting for audience participatory theatre / Jeff Wirth.
            p.   cm.
      Includes bibliographical references.
      ISBN 0-9632374-9-7 : $14.95
      1. Improvisation (Acting). 2. Theater audiences. 3. Participatory theater. I. Title.
PN2071.I5W57 1994   94-25482
692' .028—dc20   CIP

Printed in the United States of America

Text and cover printed on recycled, acid-free paper

Fall Creek Press
Post Office Box 1127
Fall Creek, OR 97438
503-744-0938

"Wait. I will walk with you."

Contents

INTRODUCTION

When you get right down to it, all theatre is interactive. Any form of theatre requires an audience with whom the performers interact. What is it, then, that distinguishes between traditional theatre and interactive theatre?

In traditional theatre the audience assumes a *reactive* role, responding to the performance in a passive fashion. Interactive theatre expands the experience of the audience by offering them a *proactive* role, in which they are invited to join as a collaborator in the creation of the performance.

Interactive theatre combines the richness of rehearsed material, the spontaneity of improvisation, and the empowerment of participation. It draws on acting and improvisation techniques, as well as skills and techniques unique to the interactive form.

This book is an overview of concepts and techniques fundamental to interactive theatre. It can serve as an introduction for those new to the field and as a brush-up review for the most experienced interactors.

The play is the thing

The element common to all forms of inter-active theatre is a sense of play. While play is frequently lighthearted and humorous, it does not exclude the possibility of serious or dramatic elements. In fact, interactive theatre can move audiences in ways that traditional theatre cannot. Why? Surprisingly, because it has the potential to feel more real.

An interactive performance does not rely on the "suspension of disbelief." It calls for an "investment of belief." The experience seems real to an audience because they are making an active investment of their minds, bodies, and spirits. When the audience become players, they are moved, because they are not just observing the performance; they are living it as well.

To achieve this kind of impact on an audience requires skill and technique. Interactive theatre demands just as much of its performers as does the traditional stage, but with one significant difference: Every successful interactive performance is created and shared by audience and performers alike. If the idea of actors, authors, technicians, designers, directors, and audience members all joining together to become playful collaborators appeals to you, read on.

The techniques and skills of both traditional and improvisational theatre have been explored in many other books. This handbook utilizes many improvisational terms developed by Keith Johnstone. While not all improvisation is interactive, Johnstone's concepts serve as a foundation upon which to build new techniques for the new genre of interactive theatre. The chapters dealing with traditional and improvisational theatre are included here as a backdrop for understanding the unique challenges and specific techniques of interactive acting.

A scan of the Table of Contents, a read-through of the chapter on Interactive Styles, a review of the Glossary, and careful attention to the chapter on Interacting will give a quick insight into what is familiar and what is unique in this challenging performance form.

Welcome to the world of interactive theatre.

INTERACTIVE STYLES

Interactive theatrical styles are constantly evolving, until today there is a wide variety of interactive performance styles. One popular style could be classified as environmental, in which the actual physical setting is used for its "reality value." Examples of this form include such commercially successful ventures as "Tony 'n Tina's Wedding" and many participatory murder mystery shows. Some interactive work has affinities to psychodrama. A recognized example of this style is Playback Theatre, developed by Jonathan Fox. Some interactive is focused on effecting social and political change. The socio-political style is well represented by the work of Augusto Boal. Yet another interactive style is Theatrical Freestyle, a form developed by Jeff Wirth, in which audience members join actors on stage to play roles in full-length shows. On the following pages you will find examples of each of these four styles.

Environmental Theatre

I'm going to see a show called "Gypsy Caravan." The ticket has all the usual information on it: date, time, price, name of the show. But along with it comes a flyer. On the flyer is a map showing where to come to see the show. It's not a theatre; it's the parking lot of a school. I'm supposed to show up at the flagpole at 2:00 o'clock. The flyer tells me to wear comfortable clothes and good walking shoes, because to see the show I will have to walk along a horse trail. The flyer also says something about audience participation, but I'm not going to get up and do anything, I'm just coming to see the show.

I arrive at the parking lot at 2:00. There's a group of people over by the flagpole, so I must be at the right place. I walk over and look around. Most of the other people have flyers like mine. Some of them are wearing hats, scarves, or skirts, that look like costumes. Was I supposed to bring a costume? The flyer didn't say anything about . . .

"Are you here for the Gypsy Caravan?"

I look up. It's a young woman in a full gypsy outfit. I nod my head and hold out my ticket.

"Thanks." She starts to rummage around in a big bag she is wearing over her shoulder, then pulls out a multicolored vest with lots of pockets and hands it to me. "Your name is Akis, and you are the cunning thief of your band of gypsies. I'll be giving some instructions to the whole group in just a few minutes."

Other people seem to be putting on costume pieces they have been given, so I put on the vest. An older man, wearing a leather hat that seems to be part of a costume, turns to me. "I don't know what I'm supposed to do here, do you?"

Grateful to find another lost soul, I say, "No, I don't either," and we commiserate about our mutual uncertainty. I learn that he is "Ramus, the leader of the band." I tell him that I am "Akis, the thief."

The girl in the gypsy outfit stands up on a box and gathers all of us around her. She welcomes us and introduces herself as Caroline. She will be playing the part of Tasha, the horse trainer from the Marcos band. She explains that the actors will play members of the Marcos band and we, the audience, will be the members of the Ramus band. The story is set in 1939 in Germany. Both of our bands are trying to get out of Germany, and we are meeting along the way to celebrate the marriage of a young man from the Marcos band and a young woman from our band. Caroline tells us that we need to be careful, because if we are captured by the Nazis, we will be sent to the camps.

She has us stand in a circle and asks us all to tell what our gypsy names are and what we do. After that, she tells us that we can participate in any way that seems appropriate. "Feel free to do things that will change the story, and try to play within the reality of the story." She tells us that the whole show will take place along the horse trails and that we will get back to the flagpole in about three hours.

She asks if we have any questions, and somebody says, "How do we know what to say?" She tells us that since we all have jobs or positions within our band, we might talk about that, or we might talk about things that have happened in our lives, or we can make up anything we'd like.

A young man standing next to me asks, "What if my mom can't keep up?" His mother whacks him one, everybody laughs, and Caroline says they will try to take a pace that will be comfortable for everyone. She says that if it gets too fast, just tell her, and she will see that everyone slows down a bit.

She asks if there are any more questions, and everybody seems satisfied, so she says,

"When you hear the bell ring, we will all be gypsies in Germany in the 1930's. And that's how everyone will remain until the bell rings again at the end of the show."

It's quiet for a moment, and then, off in the distance, we hear a bell ringing. Suddenly, here comes a whole other band of gypsies, singing and laughing and waving. Caroline calls out, "Let's go!" and we all follow her over to a grassy area across the street. I stay pretty close to Ramus, since he's the only person I know.

Just as the two groups come together, up walks this big guy with a bushy beard, who tells us he is leader of the other band. He throws his arm around Ramus and asks him if he ever sold that lame horse. Ramus hesitates, then tosses back, "Yeah, but I didn't get as much money as I hoped." Marcos glances over at me and says, "A pity. But I would wager you got the rest of the money using someone else's skills, right?" "Oh . . . oh, yeah," Ramus says, "our thief stole the rest of the money." Marcos turns to me. "Ever the nimble fingers, eh?" I nod my head. "I have a job to talk with you about later on," he says to me, "but first, I have some business with everyone."

With that, he jumps up on a rock and gets everybody's attention. As he talks about the upcoming wedding, I begin to figure out who the members of his band are, too. Then we all give a big cheer for the bride and groom and head off down the horse trail.

Pretty soon I notice that that young man's mother is telling a story about our band. She's doing a pretty good job, too. I figure I could never do that. But a little later I meet a shy young girl named Kachenka and suddenly I find myself promising to set her up with a guy from our band. By the time we stop for the wedding, I'm really getting into it. I hold the branches over the heads of the bride and groom, and when the wedding is over, I tell the bride I'm going to miss her when our bands separate.

We're all sitting under a big weeping willow tree, drinking toasts to the bride and groom, when a couple of renegade soldiers come over the hill. They try to break up the party, but I manage to steal their guns, and the rest of our band overpowers them. Ramus interrogates them, and it turns out they're not such bad guys after all. In fact, they decide to stay on and travel with us.

We have all kinds of other adventures. Once, we have to secretly get across this long wooden bridge without being spotted by Nazi soldiers. Later, we steal some eggs from a farm and have to escape from the farmer with his shotgun and his dogs.

Finally, we come to a place where the trail divides. Marcos tells us that his band is going to turn east—they're heading for the safety of Russia. Since our band is going on north, we know we probably won't be seeing each other again. Marcos gives me a gift of some wooden dice that he has carved, and I find myself getting a little misty eyed. We stand there and watch as the Marcos band disappears down the trail. It is very quiet; you can hear a couple of birds, and then, off in the distance, the sound of a bell ringing.

Caroline comes back then and leads us through some trees. There, on a paved road, a bus is waiting for us. As we ride back to the parking lot, everyone is talking about all the things that happened to us on the trail. When we get to the flagpole, there is the cast, waiting for us, and we get a chance to talk to them as real people. An hour later, I'm still there in the parking lot, talking with a few cast and audience members. It doesn't seem possible that just three hours ago we were all strangers.

Playback Theatre

My friend, Doug, and I have learned that the local Playback Theatre Company will be performing at a nearby community center. We have enjoyed their work several times in the past, so we get tickets and make plans to go.

We have never been inside Weathers Hall before, but the low, raised platform "stage," with its prop tree draped with colored scarves and the six boxes across the back, is familiar. We sit in curved rows of chairs, facing the stage. Across the way are some "regulars" that we've seen at other Playback performances. We also see some nervous first-timers.

Showtime arrives and the musician starts playing. When he finishes, six performers come in through a side door and sit on the boxes. The conductor welcomes us to the show and explains that Playback Theatre is a place for playing out stories that have been significant in our lives. Then she says, "Well, it's the holiday season. How are you feeling about the approaching festivities?"

I raise my hand, and the conductor picks me. "I dread the influx of my whole family. I can hardly wait for the holidays to be over." She asks my name, and I say, "Chris."

"Thank you, Chris. Watch."

One of the actors steps to the center of the stage and looks furtively around. The piano plays some ominous music, and suddenly, all the other actors converge on the one in the center in a screaming, babbling dogpile. Then they rush back to their boxes, as quickly as they came, leaving the center person prostrate on the floor. The piano plays a final chord. There's a pause. The conductor asks, "Did that capture your feeling, Chris?"

"It sure did."

Then the conductor asks the audience, "Does someone have a different feeling about the approaching holidays?" Several other audience members state their feelings, and their responses are also played back in fluid sculptural forms, usually ending with everyone in a sculptural freeze.

After several of these sculptures, the conductor tells us that now we're going to move on to stories. She explains that the stories can be about anything from their lives—something that has happened that day, something from a long time ago, anything of which we were a part. There is an uncomfortable silence. Doug volunteers. The conductor invites him to come forward, and he is seated on a chair at the side of the stage, beside the conductor.

The conductor asks what Doug's story is about. Doug tells about a time when the school bully took his bike away from him.

"Who would you like to play you?"

Doug points at the short, blond-haired actor, sitting on the second box. He stands up.

"And the bully?"

Doug picks a heavy-set, balding actor, who also stands.

With the conductor's support, Doug finishes the story of how he couldn't keep the bully from banging up his bike and getting off scot free when the principal arrived. When he finishes, the conductor turns to the audience and says, "Here is Doug's story about feeling helpless in the face of brute force. Watch."

The musician starts to play a tune that evokes playful memories, as the actors silently take positions on the stage and the "bully" wraps a red scarf around his forehead. The actors seem ready and positioned, the music stops, and the scene begins.

We see the actor who is playing Doug arrive at school, happily pedaling his "bike" which is another actor. The scene is both comic and awful, as the bully intimidates "Doug," forces him off his bike, and then sets about beating the bike into a twisted lump. When the principal arrives, the bully's presence keeps "Doug" from telling who damaged his bike. The bully goes off laughing.

All the players freeze for a moment. Then they turn and look questioningly and respectfully to Doug. The conductor asks, "Did that capture your story, Doug?" He nods thoughtfully. Perhaps it captured more for him than I realize.

"Thank you for starting off our evening with your story, Doug." As my friend makes his way back to his seat, he receives smiles from various audience members, and the woman in the seat on the other side of him pats his knee when he sits down.

"Who else has a story to tell?" This time hands go up quickly, and throughout the evening other stories follow: humorous, thought-provoking, curious, intense, fanciful; creating a tapestry of experiences and understandings—some shared by the audience as a whole and some intensely personal.

Two hours have gone by very quickly, many people still have stories they want to tell, and we have not grown tired of hearing them, but now the conductor is asking us for themes that have shown up in the stories of the evening.

"A sense of humor will get you through most anything." "The world isn't always fair." "People will help if you just ask." "Never drink coffee after 2:30."

The conductor turns to the cast, the music starts, and one of the players takes center stage and begins the conclusion of the show, a distillation of the themes in words and visual images. "Sometimes it hurts to laugh," he says. Another player stands up and positions the speaker in a chair, legs splayed, head thrown back, hands grasping his stomach.

Now the speaker speaks again. "I wish I weren't alone." The other player repositions the speaker, pulling his knees together, body hunched forward in a seated fetal position.

"And sometimes I'm not." The "sculptor" stretches out the speaker's arms in a large crescent and glances upstage. Suddenly, we see an idea flash in the other players' eyes. One by one they rise and extend their arms in encompassing crescents as well. The piano plays a satisfying chord and the show is over.

Doug and I will be back again. We both have more stories to tell.

Theatre of the Oppressed - Forum Theatre

The play is coming to an end and we are only twenty minutes into the show. The performers have presented a story in which an independent, free-thinking university student named Diane is being coerced by her philosophy professor into conformity of thought and behavior. We have seen a progression of scenes: One in which the professor shames her into silence in class; another in which she goes to her parents for advice; and one in which she is talking with her friends over coffee. The play ends with Diane leaving school and applying for a position with a temp agency.

At the conclusion of this rather depressing scenario, the Joker, who is a sort of master of ceremonies, informs us that the play will be presented once again, exactly as we have seen it before. If we don't want it to be played out in precisely the same way, he says we should watch for any time when we think Diane could do something differently, and at that point we can call out, "Stop." We are then to come up on stage, take on the role of Diane, and try our different strategy.

The play begins again, and we're a good five minutes into it. Diane has already been oppressed several times, and still no one has stopped the show. When the professor again uses sarcasm in front of the class to put down her point of view, a young woman in the front row finally can't take it any longer and calls out, "Stop." The Joker goes to her and the audience member says, "She shouldn't let him get away with that."

Motioning to the stage, the Joker says, "Show us what you have in mind."

"Well, she should . . ."

"No, don't tell us. Come up and show us, by playing Diane."

The young woman walks up on stage, and the actor playing Diane takes off her poncho and puts it on the audience member. "Where do you want us to take it from?"

"Where the professor made that sarcastic comment."

The scene starts again with the professor's sarcastic line. The new Diane makes a valiant effort to defend her position.

"Well, my dear, your thoughts would certainly be valuable . . . in a nursery school."

"I don't think you should talk to me that way."

"When you have a Ph.D., I'd be very interested in knowing your thoughts. But until then, it doesn't really much matter to me what you think."

This exchange continues until even some of the students are giving Diane dirty looks and whispering for her to sit down. Finally, she sits down.

Now another audience member calls out "Stop," becomes the new Diane, and jumps into the scene in which she talks with her parents. This time she convinces them to file a complaint with the school, but when the meeting occurs, the administration stonewalls, and nothing changes.

Throughout the evening various audience members attempt other strategies, some more successful than others. As Diane's strategies for dealing with the professor become more effective, the Joker invites audience members to replace actors playing other characters, and other forms of oppression are revealed. By the end of the evening we have reached no ultimate solutions, but we have gained insight and we have plenty of new courses of action to consider. We adjourn to a nearby coffee shop and heated and passionate discussions continue for several hours after the show.

Theatrical Freestyle

I had been to the show last Saturday. That was my first time to see a Theatrical Freestyle show. Now that I knew how it worked, I thought I could get much more out of the show, so I decided to come back again.

The cast members were scattered throughout the auditorium, mingling with the audience, the same as before. I waved to the actress who would be playing the role of Helen and she smiled back. I took my seat. As I continued to watch her, I realized that she was choosing the audience member who would be playing the lead role of her husband Bob. So that was how it happened. I had wondered. About that time, another member of the cast came up and started chatting with me, and I remained so engaged until the pre-show began.

The pre-show information seemed much easier to digest this second time around. It was again presented by a man that I knew would serve in the show as a sort-of narrator, commentator, and director. He invited the audience to participate by coming up to him during the show and telling him what plot developments we would like to see as the show progressed. He also explained the "On Deck" sign, a sign which lights up during the show to indicate how many audience performers, otherwise known as spect-actors, are needed for upcoming scenes. He finished by assuring us that we didn't need to be actors to participate, that it was the actors' job to make us look good.

There was a buzz of nerves, excitement, and anticipation, as the lights dimmed, the music swelled, and the curtain rose on the first scene of the play. It was the courtship between Helen and Bob at the Frances Cafe, and, while it was familiar, it took on very different dimensions from a similar scene in last week's show. It was difficult to tell if the scene was scripted, because I recognized some of the lines from last Satur-day, but much of the dialogue was different. The blocking was different, too. And while the scene still moved the story in basically the same direc-tion as last week, the way the audience member playing Bob performed created overtones that were very different from last Saturday.

The show was partway into the second scene when I noticed that the On Deck sign was on and that they needed two men and three women for some upcoming scenes. I wasn't going to wait until the second act to get involved, like last time, so I got up, excused my way down my row to the aisle, and walked to the On Deck area in front of the right-hand corner of the stage. There, a cast member was quietly telling the man and woman ahead of me that they would be playing the cook and waitress at the Frances Cafe. The actress then turned to me and told me that in a later scene I would be playing the role of Principal Becker, and all I needed to know was that I had expelled a student named Marci for being a trouble-maker. Aside from that, I was to play the scene however I liked. Then we were taken up on stage and seated with the rest of the cast on benches that lined the right and left sides of the stage.

The cafe scene went well, and as the couple who had played the cook and waitress made their way back to their seats, they were all smiles. One of the people dressed in black, a sort-of invisible stage hand, came over and led me to the chair behind my desk. Suddenly, the lights were on and one of my teachers was complaining to me that she didn't want Helen, who, it turned out, was a probation officer, to be able to dictate that Marci be re-admitted to her class. I informed the teacher that I would not let anyone tell me how to run my school.

I then turned to Helen to hear her side, knowing full well that she would try to play on my sympathies to get Marci re-admitted. Just as Helen was finishing her plea, my secretary brought in Marci's file. Now I was going to let her have it. I pointed to all the violations that were written in Marci's record (they actually *were* written there in the file on my desk), and I told Helen that that kind of girl doesn't belong in school; she belongs in juvenile hall.

Helen tried to argue the point, but I wouldn't budge. I was the principal and my say was final. My real reason was that in last week's performance the audience member playing the principal had re-admitted Marci, and I wanted to see what would happen to the story if she wasn't allowed back in school. I signed a paper indicating my refusal, and as the teacher gave a superior nod of satisfaction, the lights switched to a scene on the other side of the stage. One of the stage-hands helped me off the stage, and I hurried back to my seat to see what would happen with the change in the story.

It was interesting to see how some scenes were nearly the same as the last performance, but some were quite different, because of who was playing them or what had happened differently. And some of the scenes were completely new, showing characters and events that gave a whole new perspective to a story I thought I already knew.

When later in the story we learned that Marci had run away and was found beaten and raped, I felt an odd twinge of responsibility. But not for long, because by that time Helen was running into a spate of bad luck with her church. My neighbor leaned over and said to me, "What more could happen to her—cancer?" After a bit of convincing that it was all right to do it, my neighbor was up whispering to the narrator that maybe Helen should be diagnosed with cancer. He had barely got back to his seat when we saw Helen start to exhibit symptoms. And by the second act, sure enough, she had been diagnosed with cancer and played the final scenes of the show from a wheelchair.

It was an unusual experience. By the end of the evening, over thirty "spectactors" had played major roles, supporting roles, and extras in the show. In many ways it was the same show, but in many others it was not.

Now that I know more about how this interactive stuff works, I have some new ideas about what could take place in this show. Maybe I'll catch it next Saturday to see what happens.

ACTING

Interactive performing begins with the ability to act. This section is not meant to teach you the art of acting. If you are an experienced actor, you already know the techniques. If you are just starting out, there are already too many books and teachers ready to help you.

The next few pages are simply to prime the pump and get your creative juices flowing. You will find there is not enough space to write essay answers to the acting questions that follow. That is not coincidental. Just make brief notes. That's all you need. Then let your imagination and memory fill in the rest.

Do you have your #2 pencil sharpened and ready? Good. You may begin.

Character

Create your character. What elements help define you as an individual?

What is your name?

_____

What is your occupation?

_____

How old are you?

_____

What type of person are you?

_____

What do you look like?

_____

How do you move physically?

_____

What are your desires?

_____

What excites you?

_____

What do you love?

_____

What do you hate?

_____

What frightens you?

_____

Whom do you control?

_____

Who controls you?

_____

What are you proud of?

_____

What are you ashamed of?

_____

What secrets do you know?

_____

You get three wishes. What are they?

_____

Environment

Now that you know who you are, where are you? What conditions surround and affect you?

In what country, state, and city do you live?

_____

Where do you work?

_____

What class of society are you a part of?

_____

Why are you in this environment?

_____

What rules of etiquette do you follow?

_____

What are your religious beliefs?

_____

What does a normal day consist of for you?

_____

How do you get your bed and board?

_____

What political system governs you?

_____

What rules do you break?

_____

How does the weather affect your life?

_____

How do you measure time and money?

_____

In what setting are you most at ease?

_____

In what setting are you most uncomfortable?

_____

Where do you eat, sleep, and keep your valuables?

_____

What in your life troubles you most?

_____

Where do you wish you were, and why?

_____

Summary

Knowing the answers to the questions in the acting section is only the beginning. These questions do not even begin to scratch the surface of things you should know. In fact, if you answer them well, your answers will raise additional questions for you to answer about your character and your environment.

The value of these questions is not in *knowing* the answers; it is in *living* the answers. The audience is not there to be impressed by your knowledge of facts about your character and environment. They want to be swept away by a character who is so believable that they can relate with you as a "real" human being in a "real" setting. The key to transforming yourself from an encyclopedia of facts into a living character in a real world is this:

OUT OF THE BRAIN,
INTO THE BODY

The value of the acting questions is not in the answers alone. The real value comes when you translate your answers into something that the audience can perceive in you physically, mentally, and emotionally.

I'm a blacksmith.

So what? Who cares?

I'm a blacksmith named Bartukus. I have huge, bulging forearms from hefting my hammer all day. I like the smell of wild flowers, because it clears my head of the stinking fumes from the forge. Sometimes I talk too loud, because I am partly deaf from the constant noise in my shop. I treat people in an extra friendly manner to make up for the fact that I can't hear every word they say. I am afraid I am getting too old to find anyone to marry; and besides, who would want to have an ugly-faced rogue like me for a husband anyway?

Now there's a character that has all kinds of life built into it. So go to it!

IMPROVISING

Interactive theatre is not just improvising. A talented improvisor is not necessarily a great interactor. That is because many improvisors are used to performing with other improvisors, not with members of the audience.

Still, a good interactor must be a consummate improvisor, whether creating a scene with a fellow interactor or with a spectactor (a member of the audience who has now become a performer in the show). Improvisational techniques establish a common language through which cooperative story building can take place.

In this chapter the "Basics" section introduces the building blocks of improvisation and covers the right and wrong way to respond to them. The "Narrative" section shows how to transform offers into scenes and stories; and "Structure" provides tools that will enhance the development, flow, and shape of the narrative.

Basics

"Let's play Army."
"O.K. Bang, you're dead."
"No I'm not."
"You are so."
"Am not."
"Are so."
"Not."
"So."
"NOT!"
"SO!"

When you improvise, you are inventing a story while acting it out. How do you do that?

As our two soldiers have demonstrated in the dialogue above, inventing a story together can be a difficult experience. Fortunately, there are techniques that make the collaborative process of improvisation easier.

This section introduces the basic skills on which all improvisational work is built. The examples given are primarily dialogue. Keep in mind, however, that a skilled improvisor communicates through actions as much as—sometimes more than—through words.

Offers

Offer: anything that a person says or does.

Offers are the building blocks from which all improvisation is built.

The scenes and stories of improvisation grow out of the clues and information sent and received through offers. There are two ways to make offers.

Verbal offer: "We're ready for our check."

Physical offer: Signaling the waiter that you are ready for your check.

Intentional Offers

An intentional offer is anything said or done to communicate information to another actor.

"Good afternoon, Mister Johnson. Here's the lamp that you ordered last Friday."

Blind Offers

Everything that anyone says or does is a potential offer. Things done without conscious intent are called blind offers.

A blind offer can be anything from the position in which a person is sitting to the fact that she is scratching her ear.

Endowment

The strongest way to present an offer is to imply the information rather than broadcast it. The way to do this is by endowing. You endow by relating to an object, a person, or a situation as though they had certain qualities. It is your relationship that communicates the information.

> *Offer: The person you are about to see is your domineering boss.*
>
> *Endowment: You tap tentatively on the office door, wait, then open the door hesitantly. Still standing in the doorway, you look at the ground and say, "You wanted to see me about the Goldblatt account, Mrs. Pemler?"*

Wimping

When you make a vague, undefined offer, you are wimping. Don't be a wimp.

> *"Boy, look at that. Isn't that something? I've never seen anything like that."*

All right already, what is it? Stop wimping. Be specific. Define your offer.

"Boy, look at that belt buckle."

Boring is interesting

Sometimes you just can't think of an offer. Well, maybe you have thought of an offer, but it's not very clever. Never mind *clever*. Don't worry about *boring*. Make the offer. Sometimes when you quit trying so hard, interesting things happen. Get on with the scene.

Basics

Blocking

Block: to undermine the truth or intent of an offer

If offers are the building blocks of improvisation, blocking is the wrecking ball. When an offer is made, it communicates information and intent.

> *Offer: (ominously) "Miss Jones, I'm ready to extract your teeth."*
>
> *Information: A dentist and Miss Jones, here for tooth extraction.*
>
> *Intent: The imminent extraction will be a terrifying experience.*

An offer gets messed up when it is blocked—when the truth of the offer is undermined, or when the direction that the offer wants to take the story is ignored.

The most common mistake of a beginning improvisor is to block offers. There are three reasons that people block.

Blocking out of Fear

When someone makes an offer, you frequently don't know where it is going to lead and whether or not you will be able to handle it. By blocking the offer, you prevent it from going anywhere, keeping yourself safe . . . and the scene stagnant.

>   *Offer: (ominously) "Miss Jones, I'm ready to extract your teeth."*
>
>   *Block: "I'm not Miss Jones."*

Blocking for Control

When you make an offer, you probably know where you want it to lead. When another performer makes a subsequent offer that doesn't fit with where you wanted to go, you may be tempted to block. Don't. You're only putting a speed bump in the scene.

>   *Your offer consists of sitting, reading, as if you were in a library. Your partner, who obviously doesn't know a library from a waiting room, enters and speaks to you.*
>
>   *Offer: (ominously) "Miss Jones, I'm ready to extract your teeth."*
>
>   *Block: "I'm sorry, I thought this was the library."*

Don't block to maintain control. Go along with your partner's offer. It may work out even better than your original idea.

Blocking for Laughs (Gagging)

Gagging is using an offer for its laugh value alone. "Hey, if the audience is laughing, what's the problem?" The problem is that the gagging prevents the scene from going anywhere, and a scene going nowhere eventually ceases to be entertaining or funny. There is nothing wrong with getting a laugh, but it should never be at the expense of the narrative.

Offer: (ominously) "Miss Jones, I'm ready to extract your teeth."

Block: "Thank goodness. My dentures have been lodged in this apple for over a week."

Basics

Accepting

Accept: to affirm the truth and intent of an offer

Accepting is not a great moral virtue in and of itself; it just makes it faster and easier to tell a story. The act of accepting says, "Yes, these story elements (offers) are true, so now we can use them as part of our story."

The most fundamental way of accepting is simply to agree.

"You have a booger in your nose."

"Oh my goodness, you're right."

As with offers, accepting does not have to be verbal. Find a physical way to demonstrate that what has been offered is true.

You pull out a handkerchief and blow the booger from your nose.

Basics
Building

Build: to make an offer that supports and expands a previous offer.

Agreeing with an offer allows an offer to stand, but a stronger way to accept an offer is to do a build. You do this by adding information that is consistent with the information and intent communicated through the previous offer.

Building makes it easier for your partner to play, because it gives her more information with which to work.

Offer: "You've got a booger in your nose."

Build: "Oh my god! And I just came from an interview with the Vice President."

The improvisor accepted that she had a booger in her nose. She added information that made the first offer consequential by offering that she had been unaware of the booger presence during an interview with the Vice President.

<u>Basics</u>
Give and Take

Have you ever done the sidewalk dance? You encounter an on-coming pedestrian. You both step to one side, you both step to the other side, and you only stay in each other's way? That's bad give and take.

It is easy to get caught up in "What am I going to do?" and totally miss what a fellow improvisor has already done. Once players get comfortable with making offers, "giving" doesn't seem to be a problem. "Taking" is another story altogether.

Taking is the ability to not only look, but see; to not only listen, but hear. These are the skills of a great improvisor. The better the give and take, the more subtle the offers can become. It can be like working in a good mentalist act. The audience doesn't see the information passing back and forth, but they see the performers responding to it. Top-notch give and take creates sub-scene communication. It allows you to know where another player is going, what she wants you to do, and even where she would like the scene to go.

So how to practice good give and take?

Pay attention to your partners

It is amazing how many offers are missed simply because the players are paying more attention to themselves than they are to each other. Remember, interacting is a cooperative venture.

Take turns

After you have made an offer, leave room for the other players to accept and build. After they've done their do, it's your turn again. Taking turns may sound a bit childish, but it is a surprisingly effective means of accomplishing good give and take.

Stop talking

If you have said more than two sentences, you may have said too much already. Be quiet, and see what other players want to say or do.

Become a detective

Watch for clues—words, facial expressions, body language. Pay attention to what your partner is trying to communicate to you through subtle offers rather than blatant words and actions.

Build on what they offer

Don't be like the party-goer who asks your opinion and then continues with his own point of view, ignoring your response. Let your brilliance shine as you enhance the offers made by your partner.

Narrative

Narrative is the story.

Books allow readers to imagine stories. Storytellers allow listeners to envision stories. Theatre allows audiences to observe stories. And interactive theatre allows audiences to participate within stories. But first you have to have a story.

There are two ways in which a story can be created improvisationally. One is playing off a scenario, such as those used in the *commedia dell'arte*. A scenario may include information on the location, the characters, and plot points. It provides a structure within which a story may be improvised.

But there are also times when improvisors (and interactors) are working from a "blank slate"—without any predetermined information that will help them create the story. Sometimes it is only a short scene, sometimes it is a full-length play.

So how do you play a story if you don't even know what it's going to be about? In this section you will learn how to create a story from a blank slate.

First, C.R.O.W. will give you landmarks by which to gauge your progress through any story. Then, pegs, links, and reincorporation will provide the freedom to discover a story as you go along.

Narrative
C.R.O.W.

The first thing to do when creating narrative is give 'em the bird—the CROW. C.R.O.W. stands for Character, Relationship, Objective, and Where.

Character

Character covers who the people are, what they do, and what types of personalities they have. Give them names, occupations, physicalities—all the things that make up a character.

Relationship

The relationship affects how each character behaves in his dealings with the other characters and the environment. Some relationships are defined by structures, such as family (brother/sister) or work (boss/employee). But any relationship becomes richer when defined by status (intimidated boss/aloof employee.) And remember that relationships also exist between characters and the environment (a child curious about a police station).

Objective

The objective introduces action into the narrative by defining what the characters want. By trying to fulfill these desires, the characters become active. When generating an objective, it is helpful to think of hands (to do something), head (to think something), and heart (to feel something). This can be useful in defining your own character.

Hands: I want to buy that pool table.

Head: "I want to convince myself that I am good-looking."

Or you can set an objective by applying it to other characters.

Heart: I want to make him despise me.

By trying to fulfill an objective, a character is moved to action within the scene.

Where

The where is the location or the environment in which the scene takes place. When the where is overlooked, the characters have no way to relate to the physical surroundings, and they may fall victim to the dreaded disease of "talking heads." (More on this later.)

Narrative

Pegs

Peg: a story element within the narrative

When improvising, we dive into a story without knowing where it will go or how it will end. We don't even know what story elements it will contain. That's why we need pegs—those story elements that turn blank minds and an empty stage into an interesting story. A peg can be anything: an object, a character, a feeling, a concept. Anything.

A story is built out of a series of pegs, that are generated on the fly and introduced into the story through offers. Pegs are generated by association. There are two types of association and they serve two different purposes.

Periphery association

To do a periphery is to come up with pegs that are related to a central topic. This is a linear skill, and very useful for generating offers that reinforce the detail of a narrative.

Topic: Wool

Periphery pegs: Shears, sheep, caps, scratchy, blanket, white, card, export, weave, dye, shepherd, mammoth.

Free association

Free association creates pegs that are unrelated to the central topic. Why do we need unrelated elements in a narrative that is supposed to make some kind of sense? Because the most interesting stories are those that contain unpredictable elements.

There are plenty of exercises for building your free-associative skills during rehearsals. But what are you supposed to do in the middle of a performance? Stop for a quick game of Firing Line? Here are a couple of ways to generate free-associative pegs, even when you're in the middle of a show.

Lazy Anagrams: Look at a nearby object. Now rearrange some of the letters in its name to make a new word. That's your peg.

> *You see a leash. You rearrange it to "shell." (Sure, there's an extra "l" and the "a" didn't get used. But who cares? It's a lazy anagram, and you've got your peg.)*

Rhymers: Think of a word that rhymes with the last word spoken. That's your peg.

"You're just out of luck." Your peg is "duck."
Or "truck." Or whatever rhyme comes to
mind. (Remember, it's a family show.)

Pegs into offers

So now you've got a peg. How is that supposed to become a part of the story? Turn it into
an offer. Introduce it as a prop in the scene. Say a
line that contains the word. Make the word a
part of your character's objective.

Peg: Reflect

Possible offers: You pull a mirror from a
drawer, saying, "I'd like to reflect on that for a
while," or you take on the same body position
as your scene partner, or you throw a penny
into a reflecting pool.

<u>Narrative</u>
Links

Link: to tie an unrelated story element into the existing narrative.

Quick, think of a word that begins with the last letter of your first name. That's your first peg. Open the book nearest to you and point to a word at random. That's your second peg. Think of a way in which the two pegs could be tied together in a scene. Congratulations. You've just made a link.

The process of creating a story begins with the linking of various story elements. Let's start a story?

Peg #1: Fur

A fur mink stole is tossed from a burning building to a fireman, who catches it down below.

Not much of a story, but it's a start. Another peg.

(Hmm. The story is at the scene of a fire. What else would be there? Ah ha! I've got it . . .)

Peg: Firehose

Yes, that's a peg, but don't worry about coming up with something that will fit well in the story. Use an arbitrary element that is unrelated to the scene, a free-associative peg. Pick another peg, unrelated to the story.

> *Marshmallow. (No, that has too obvious a connection to fire.)*

> *Girdle. (No, that probably relates to the woman whose fur was tossed from the window.)*

Relax. Turn off that little editor's voice in your head. As long as you weren't *trying* to think of a peg that would fit in the story, that's all that matters. If, after the fact, you see how the peg could easily be linked to the story, so much the better.

> *Peg: Milk*

> *Link: As the fireman turns to go back to the street with the coat in his hands, he trips over a bottle of milk left on the porch.*

Another peg now, and link it to the preceding peg.

> *Peg: Calm*

Link: As the shattered milk bottle spills its contents on the walk, a calico cat walks calmly up, ignoring the commotion of the fire, and serenely laps up the milk.

That's a pretty interesting story so far, but something is missing. Something that will make a series of linked pegs start to feel more like a story. Something like . . . Reincorporation.

Narrative

Reincorporation

Reincorporation: linking an element brought up earlier in the narrative to the current situation.

Reincorporation is similar to linking, except you don't have to generate new information. You tie old information to the present situation.

Let's go back to the story of "The Fireman and the Cat."

Reincorporate: Fur

The calico cat finishes its milk, then turns and leaps into the arms of the fireman, snuggling down comfortably in the fur coat.

A woman with a mud pack still drying on her face comes running out of the crowd. "My precious Boopsie. You saved her. Oh, you wonderful man!"

A series of linked pegs can make perfect sense but still not be satisfying, because they seem to have no point. People like stories to have a point. When reincorporation occurs, we think "Oh, now I get it." Don't ask me why. Perhaps because life sometimes feels like a series of linked pegs, and we're hoping there's some purpose to it all in the end.

But back to the issue at hand. Random pegs keep the progression of a story less predictable. Reincorporation creates a sense of purpose to the progression by creating interrelationships between the story elements.

So that's how to evolve a narrative and discover a story: Keep linking unrelated pegs until you have a substantial quantity of raw material; then start reincorporating.

Structure

"Structure? We don't need no stinking structure. We make it up as we go along."

Some improvisors shy away from structure because it seems too premeditated, contrary to the spontaneous creation of an improvised story. But can you imagine a group of jazz musicians trying to improvise without any comprehension of time signature, keys, or measures? A structure is like a good set of monkey bars. It's there not to restrict you, but, rather, to provide a framework within which to play more freely.

By understanding narrative structure, an entire cast can have a group awareness of where they are in the story and what type of things should be happening at certain times. It can help you keep the story from wandering, fizzling, or dying altogether.

An improvisor is both a player and a playwright. By understanding structure, players can create narrative, not only from the viewpoint of a character within the story, but also from the outside perspective of an author.

When structure becomes second nature, it frees the improvisor to play within the story. So let's learn some structure.

Structure
B.M.E.T

B.M.E.T. stands for Beginning, Middle, End, Tag. It can be applied to a short scene or to an entire play. Here is how it works.

Think of a character in a place.

Once upon a time there was a mouse named Buddy, who lived in an old can of tennis balls at a country club.

Think of something bad that happens to the character.

A tennis pro named Biff mistook Buddy for a tennis ball, picked him up, and smashed little Buddy across the tennis court, scoring an ace.

Resolve the bad thing that happened.

Buddy picked up his battered little body off the court and ran away to live in the eighteenth hole of a nearby golf course.

Make up a moral that relates to what happened.

Life on the courts can be rough on mice.

There you have a story. It consists of a beginning, a middle, an ending, and a tag. Here is what happens in each section.

Beginning: establish characters and setting.

Middle: make trouble.

Ending: resolve the trouble.

Tag: sum it all up.

There are many other ways to structure a story. B.M.E.T. has the advantage of being one with which most improvisors (and audiences) are familiar.

Knowing a structure is one thing. Applying the structure to an improvisational performance is another. Here are some helpful hints.

Beginning — Establish the CROW

In the beginning, the first order of business is to establish the C.R.O.W. Who is the story about, where is it happening, and what is going on? These specifics are the foundation on which the story will be built.

The beginning is also a good time to introduce elements that add texture, depth, and detail to characters and environment. At the very least, these details make the story richer, but they also provide elements that can come in handy later for reincorporation.

Middle — Find the trouble

A routine is something happening the way it always does. A story is something happening differently.

After we know the who, what, and where, something needs to happen. Or, more specifically, something out of the ordinary needs to happen. Not everything that is out of the ordinary is trouble, but it's an easy way to remember what needs to happen in the middle.

For some reason, putting themselves in trouble is very difficult for some improvisors. When trouble starts to happen, they do everything they can to stay safe. That puts a roadblock right in the way of the narrative. What's the problem? It's all pretend anyway. So relax, jump in, let trouble happen; it makes for a better story. There are lots of ways to find trouble. The next chapter is full of them.

End — Resolve the trouble

The key to resolving trouble is allowing it to be solved. Many improvisors have difficulty getting into trouble, and many can't seem to resolve the trouble once they get into it.

If the trouble is Rick's heartbreak because his favorite doll was shoved down the garbage disposal: buy him a new one, sew the old one back together, destroy the garbage disposal; just resolve the problem.

Don't forget your old friend, reincorporation. Reintroduce a story element that was offered earlier in the narrative and let it take care of the problem.

> *You have introduced Louise and Ralph Portley, doing their taxes at the kitchen table while little Rhonda plays nearby with her toys. Ralph and Louise find themselves in trouble when a robber breaks in and holds them at knife-point.*

> *The trouble is resolved when Rhonda forces the robber to surrender by intimidating him with a reincorporated toy, an amazingly realistic-looking squirt gun.*

Warning: Don't start introducing new characters or problems during the end. Stay with the information that has been established, or the story will head off in a new direction, leaving the original story still unresolved.

Tag — Sum it all up

The idea of a tag is to give a brief handle that helps the audience reflect on the story they have just seen. Here are some ways to create a tag.

Loop back to the place where it all began.

A man with a terrible slice works and works on his golf game until he wins the Palm Beach Open. After everyone has left the awards ceremony, he takes one last swing, just for fun, and slices it into the rough.

Make a miracle happen; accomplish what was being sought all through the story but never happened.

A man nearly wins the Palm Beach Open, but hooks terribly at the last hole and loses the tournament. After everyone has left the awards ceremony, he takes one last, disgusted swing . . . and makes a hole-in-one.

Turn the focus to an element from the resolution of the story.

After winning the Palm Beach Open, a man places the loving cup on his desk, cleans a smudge off the silver with his handkerchief, and sits back to admire his trophy.

Many times a tag occurs naturally. The performers need to be aware and ready to stop when the tag happens, or the story will roll right on past it.

Apply pegs, links, and reincorporation, and have your outside eye watching to see how it is all fitting in the four-sentence story structure, and you have the best of both worlds—an interesting and unpredictable story with a clear and satisfying structure.

Structure
Good Trouble

Trouble is at the heart of all good stories.

There is no story if the three little pigs each build a house and no one tries to blow the houses down. If Cinderella is born a princess, marries Prince Charming, and they live happily ever after, who cares?

You want a story? You need trouble, right here in River City. Here are some ways to find it.

Persecute the hero

Get someone in trouble. Much of life is spent trying to stay out of trouble, but stories happen when characters get into trouble. So get a character into trouble. Sexually harass your employee. Get caught buying drugs on the black market. Be late to an important interview. Lose a finger in a band saw.

Anyone can be persecuted, but it usually works better when it's the protagonist. When the antagonist gets in trouble, there is sometimes a feeling that the villain is simply getting what he deserves. Audiences prefer to see a person they care about, struggling to overcome the persecution.

Break the routine

A routine is any type of action or event that, if it goes according to plan, will be relatively predictable. It can also be the way in which the action is usually done. Brushing your teeth is a routine. (unless you don't usually brush your teeth, in which case I can recommend a good dentist). Brushing your teeth, accidentally using hair cream instead of toothpaste, breaks the routine and becomes a story. Here are some routines:

Serving beer at Marty's Tavern.
Playing basketball.
Talking softly to a sleeping baby.

To break a routine, simply put a "not" in front of the routine, and then justify why.

Not serving beer at Marty's Tavern, because ...

... the Tavern has run out of beer.

... some clumsy oaf dumped his drink all over you, and you need to change your clothes.

Not playing basketball, because ...

... a stray bullet rips through the ball, interrupting the game.

. . . as you are playing in the smog, your asthma kicks in.

Not talking softly to a sleeping baby, because . . .

. . . you start yelling at the baby for relieving itself on your silk shirt.

. . . you begin to plead fearfully with the baby when it awakens and demands your immortal soul.

Peel the onion.

Another source of good trouble lies within the character. In the beginning, you define a character with specific personality traits. You can find plenty of trouble by peeling away a layer of the character's surface and revealing a trait that is at odds with the character's image. Here's an example of how to peel an onion.

Think of a trait that identifies your character.

Bravery: You have been on an expedition with Sir Walter Raleigh. You are bragging about the dangers you faced to obtain a rare spice, which you are now trying to sell to a midwife.

Think of a trait of human nature that contradicts that characteristic.

People are afraid of the unknown.

Find a way to justify, revealing the contradictory character trait.

*The midwife is very impressed with you and
buys your spice. She offers you a drink, which
you gladly accept. After taking a huge swal-
low, you realize that the taste is unfamiliar to
you. You become deathly afraid for your life,
imagining all sorts of ill effects from the for-
eign liquid.*

Conflict — Play for the loss

Conflict is not synonymous with trouble.

One character has a ball, the other wants it.
If they both pursue their objectives, there will be
conflict, but not trouble. Trouble happens only if
one of the players permits his character to "lose."

Improvisational performers frequently
play for the "win," trying to achieve their character's objective and become the "winner."
Improvisational conflict is best created as it is in
stage combat: an illusion of conflict is presented
through the cooperative work of performers
who trust each other.

Imagine what catastrophes might transpire
if the actors playing Mercutio and Tybalt actually

tried to best each other with their swords. Yet it is not uncommon for improvisors to use their skills as weapons in an attempt to win the scene for their character. This happens when they are playing for their own personal interest rather than for the value of the overall scene.

Conflict in improvisation should be played as a cooperative sport. This doesn't mean playing your character's objectives with any less conviction. It simply means playing with your author's eye as well. Sometimes the most interesting scene will lie in the "defeat" of your character.

It is a top-notch improvisor who can provide another player the means to win a conflict while still appearing to try to win it himself. The victory is given, not taken.

So how does the winner get chosen if both performers are playing for the loss? Eventually, the momentum of the scene will begin moving the story, and the momentum of the scene will pick a winner. A structural element that can be very satisfying is for the winner to give the loser a little win tag on the end of the scene.

Detective Costello has caught Nick the Stick in a lie that is going to send him to the county lockup. Costello turns to his desk to fill out the appropriate paperwork. As he turns, his jacket rides up, clearing his back pocket, from which Nick lifts his wallet just as they cart him off.

Structure
Bad Trouble

There is trouble and then there is trouble.

Trouble that messes with the lives of characters in the story is good trouble. Trouble that interferes with the work of the performers creating the story is bad trouble.

Getting others in trouble

"Don't block; always accept the offer." That is great advice, but like any advice, it can be misused. "You have to accept my offer, whatever that offer may be" just doesn't work if you have established a reputation for putting your fellow performers in untenable positions. For performers to be comfortable accepting an offer, there must be a foundation of trust. That trust is based in the assumption that players put each other into trouble for the good of the story, not to mess with each others' heads. Here are some types of trouble to avoid.

Monkeywrenching

Introducing trouble, then sitting back and doing nothing, while watching others deal with the consequences.

"Larry, bad news. You have a degenerative bone disease that will dissolve your skull in thirty seconds."

Character breaking

Throwing an assumption for the sole purpose of forcing a player to behave in a way that violates his character.

"Your Majesty, I understand that you enjoy dancing around like a banshee on the hour. It's four o'clock."

Nailing

Making an offer for the purpose of getting the performer, rather than the character, in trouble.

"That's a nasty burn on your back. You'd better remove your blouse so I can apply the proper ointment."

The only thing wrong with those three offers is the intent behind them. Each could serve as a valuable addition to the narrative, if that were what they were intended to serve.

Part of making an appropriate offer of trouble is knowing and respecting the player you are putting in trouble. He knows you are looking out for the value of the scene, his character, and who he is in real life as well.

When you get the characters in trouble, but not the players, trust is built. Without trust, great improv can't happen.

Structure
Avoiding Action

Want to create a bad story or a boring story, or derail a good one? It's easy. Just avoid action. There are lots of ways to avoid the type of action that makes for good narrative. Learn 'em so's you don't do 'em.

Avoiding the obvious

Has the story led to a point where it is obvious to everyone what is going to happen next? Don't try to come up with something clever. Do what the story wants you to do.

> *Eric has carried his bike to the top of a steep hill. What happens next? The bike gets a flat tire? Not a chance. Bike? Steep hill? You figure it out.*

Staying safe

Are you keeping yourself out of danger? Why? Nothing is going to happen to you; it's going to happen to your character.

> *Chris is in the house where a serial killer is hiding. The lights have just gone out. Should Chris go down in the basement to check the fuse box? You betcha!*

Talking Heads

Are you talking about the action you are about to do? Are you talking about action that happened in the past? Are you talking about action that is happening somewhere else, or just off-stage? Stop talking about action—start living it.

> *"Ah, nothing like a day at the beach. I'm ready for a good swim."*
>
> *"Yes, nothing like a brisk swim to perk you up."*
>
> *"It's a good thing I brought my swim trunks. I couldn't swim without them."*
>
> *"You know, a man drowned on this beach last week."*
>
> *"Look. There's a man drowning out there right now."*
>
> *"You're right. He seems to be waving for help."*
>
> *"Maybe we should do something."*

(Yeah, like maybe do some action.)

Sidetracking

Has something happened that should be pursued? Then don't veer off in some other direction by introducing something else.

Josephine is trapped at home and longs to escape. She saves enough money for a car of her own. As she is walking to Trusty Sam's Car Emporium, she sees an auto accident and stops to help. She goes to the hospital and donates one of her kidneys to save the life of the accident victim.

What happened to Josephine's trip to the Car Emporium and her quest for freedom?

Cul-de-sacking

Is your action leading you back to exactly the place where you began? If you pursue an action, it should lead you someplace new and further progress the story.

Punky is proud of her clean kitchen. She sees droppings and becomes concerned that there may be mice in her kitchen. She empties the cupboards and checks for mice. No mice. The "droppings" were pieces of brown rice. Punky can once again be proud of her clean kitchen.

That's nice for Punky, but boring for the story.

Routines

Routines seem like action; they seem to involve doing something. But it's not the kind of action that makes for a good story unless the routine gets broken. Cooking an omelet? Playing hopscotch? We already know how most routines are done. Show us something we don't know.

"Hey batter, batter, batter, SWING!"

"Strike three, you're out."

We know. We know. When is something unexpected going to happen?

Teaching

Teaching is a very popular "action" that tends to lead nowhere. It adds insult to injury by forcing the audience to watch one player show another player how to perform a routine. Very easy, very predictable, very boring.

"No, hold your arm up a little higher. That's it. Now, one, two, cha-cha-cha."

Trouble for trouble's sake

If the point of trouble is just showing the trouble, there is no progression, and no story. The point of trouble is to move through it.

"Help! Quicksand! Someone help me! I'm sinking. Somebody throw me the vine! I can't reach it! I'm going to die!"

Newsflash: you're dying already.

Conflict Loops

Conflict is a clever way to avoid action. Play it right and it can keep you from ever having to pursue any real action. If there is conflict, move through it, not to it.

> *"I've locked Heidi in the cellar."*

> *"What are you talking about? You can't do that."*

> *"Of course I can, I'm her mother."*

> *"Well I'm her father, and I say you let her out now."*

> *"I won't have you telling me how to raise my child."*

> *"She's my child too, you know."*

> *"You'd never know it, the way you're never around."*

> *"I have to make a living don't I? I have to support the family."*

When is father going to stop beating around the bush and start looking for the key to the cellar?

Gagging

If the comedy keeps you from going to the action, it is at the expense of the story. Then you don't have a story. What's the point?

> *"Remember, soldier: Jump, count to ten, then pull the ripcord."*

> *"Wait a minute sergeant. This is my knapsack full of dirty laundry. Where's my parachute?"*

Go on, sergeant, push him out the door anyway.

<u>Structure</u>
Style

Part of what makes a story satisfying is that it is always played out within the reality of its particular narrative style.

In a fairy tale it is perfectly acceptable for a prince to become a frog. Try the same thing in an historical drama and it becomes a different style entirely. What plays as clever plot twists in a comedy simply becomes bad writing in a tragedy. It is important to remain within the "reality rules" of the narrative style in which you are performing.

Does this stifle creativity? Not at all. The wildest offer is not necessarily the most creative one. It often take more creativity to develop an interesting story from within the "reality" of a particular style.

You are delivering a clandestine letter and do not wish to be caught with it in your possession. If you were playing in a fantasy style, you might invoke a spell to make the letter vanish. But you are playing historical, so, instead, the letter has been written with disappearing ink.

INTERACTING

The element that differentiates interactive theatre from other forms of theatre is the creative participation of the audience. It draws on the techniques of acting and improvisation but focuses on the creation of an experience which can be fulfilled only through the willing collaboration of the audience.

Just as a jazz musician must first master such basics as scales and chord progressions, an interactor must first master the fundamentals of acting and improvisation. But that is only the beginning.

When you can give a great performance yourself, you're an actor or an improvisor. When you can start with people who have never stood on a stage, never made a speech, never entertained a group, and free those audience members to be great performers in their own right, then you have become an interactor.

First Contact

It is a moment for the history books.

An alien spacecraft has landed. Human beings are about to have their first contact with beings from another galaxy. And what do we hear over the headsets?

This is command base. We have visual on alien beings. All squadrons lock and load weapons, hold your positions, and be prepared to fire upon command.

In interactive theatre, the first contact with an audience is crucial. Even at their most normal, performers can seem like alien beings. Or at least like elephants. They are interesting to watch from a distance, but when they walk right up next to you, it can be a little unnerving.

The interactor's work begins long before there is even a question of the audience performing on stage. It begins with the first contact and how you relate with your audience. It is not a relationship created behind the safety of a fourth wall, but one that requires you to empathize with the thoughts and feelings of people who are used to being passive observers. (It's not a bad idea, either, to know whom to pick and how to pick them when the time comes.) It's all part of your first contact with those equally scary alien beings from the other side of the proscenium arch—spectactors.

<u>First Contact</u>

Respect

"This is good theatre. If the audience doesn't get it, that's their problem."

"If that's the kind of schlock people want, that's what we'll give them."

Neither of these attitudes respects the audience. The first makes no effort to reach the audience where they are; the other assumes that where they are is where they wish to remain. The art of any work lies in the ability to reach people where they are, while helping them stretch to what they might become. The minute we put down or write off an audience because of their response, we have ceased to respect them.

In traditional theatre it is not unusual to think of an audience that isn't responding appropriately as a "bad audience." They think the work is "bizarre" rather than "meaningful." They are not laughing, or, worse yet, they are laughing in the wrong places. They are restless, sitting on their hands, or dead. Frequently, the response to a "bad" audience seems to be, "Hey, we rehearsed this show without you. We can perform it without you, too."

In interactive theatre, to write off the audience is equivalent to writing off the director, the author, or a fellow performer. The audience is a creative collaborator, without whom there is no show. The contribution of the audience must always be respected.

True, many times the contributions of an audience in interactive theatre fall far short of the desired mark. But consider a "method trained" actor, suddenly thrust onto a Kabuki stage; the results might be less than stunning.

We can never allow ourselves to write off spectactors because of poor or inappropriate participation. We must learn to see beyond that. Spectactors must always be respected, even if their actions are not what we desire.

Respect is not just a way of thinking; it is a way of doing. You begin by stepping into the shoes of your audience, in order to understand what they think and feel.

I hope you're wearing clean socks.

<u>First Contact</u>
The "F" Word

The biggest obstacle to audience participation is the big "F" word—fear.

What are they afraid of? Looking like an idiot. Saying something stupid. Doing the wrong thing. Being inadequate.

How does their fear affect them?

Symptom #1 - no participation

These people won't play at all. I gave that guy a great offer, and all he did was sit and stare at me. If he doesn't want to participate, why did he come to an interactive show in the first place?

Symptom #2 - passive, defensive, or obnoxiously extroverted participation

It was awful. I walked up to table thirteen, introduced myself, and this big guy yells, "All right, baby!" jumps up, grabs me, and tries to kiss me.

These responses to a first approach often do not accurately reflect the participant's personality. They are defense mechanisms, used to

cope with the spectactor's immediate problem—
fear.

The interactor's first job is to eliminate that
fear. When it gets tough, remember:

They're not a bad audience; they're just scared.

First Contact
T.L.C.

Take care of your audience. To overcome their fear, they need all the care and friendship they can get.

Why all this touchy-feely stuff about care and friendship? It's pragmatic. Most spectactors are not actors. They don't know how to act, especially not in front of strangers. If they're going to take the risk of performing, they need to feel there is a friend who will help them out along the way. Guess what? You're elected. So what to *do?*

Be friendly

Smile. Look them in the eyes. Shake hands. Take them by the arm. Treat them like your friends, and they are likely to become just that.

What if you're playing a character who is rude, caustic, or otherwise unpleasant? No problem. Treat the people around you as your friends, confidants, and cronies. Let those who are out of earshot become the object of your unpleasantness.

Be interested in them

In your first contact with an audience, don't be in a hurry to start performing for them. Take time to get to know a bit about the people in your audience. Not just as a group. Get to know who individuals are by working one-on-one. This allows them to see you as a real person, even if you are relating to them in character. An audience will be more willing to trust you when they have related to you as a real person who is interested in them.

Compliment them

Have you ever been wearing some grungy old jeans when someone came up and said, "I've got to tell you, those jeans look really good on you"? It's amazing what miracles a compliment will accomplish. Find something about which you can give an honest compliment: her hair, his clothes, his personality, her wisdom, their children, her style . . . anything. If you have to, you can even bend the truth a little. That's not lying; that's flattery. A judicious compliment goes a long way toward setting people at ease and enhancing their willingness to participate.

Don't act in their faces

Remember that you are an actor. You are comfortable performing to the back of a five thousand seat auditorium. But that audience member right next to you has seen your work only from twenty-seven rows back . . . until now. Suddenly, he realizes that your voice is very strong and your facial expressions are more exaggerated than normal.

Don't let your acting be a gale force that blasts away the spectactor next to you. If he feels intimidated by your power, he's not likely to play. So perform big enough to be easily seen and heard by the rest of the audience, but not so big that it overwhelms the person you're with.

If they're hesitant . . .

If they are hesitant about relating to you, keep at it. Smile a little more. Be a little more friendly. They are almost with you.

Physical contact can be effective if it is done with an easy assurance. But don't invade their space; share it. When you see hesitancy, relax. They are almost ready to be comfortable with you.

If they're afraid . . .

If they're afraid of you, be more passive in your friendliness. Never acknowledge their fear, but don't be so quick to move into their space. It's similar to making friends with a scared puppy. When they see that you are no threat to them, they will be more willing to play.

If you have given the passive approach a fair shot and they are still fearful, sometimes a sudden shot of aggressive friendliness will break the ice. But be forewarned: this approach also runs the risk of turning their fear into terror. Let experience and intuition be your guides.

If they're terrified . . .

If they are terrified, back off. Stop relating to them directly. Find a way to relate to someone or something else, and let them watch you instead. Never try to directly overcome a spectactor's terror; it only makes the situation worse. It's like the little kid who's afraid of a clown. No matter how friendly the clown is, the longer he stays, the louder the kid cries.

Above all . . .

Keep your focus on your audience and how each person is feeling. Create good, friendly relationships with individuals. There will be plenty of time to focus on performing after they have become comfortable with you.

First Contact
Picking Spectactors

Before you can start playing with the audience, you need to know with whom you will be playing. Picking the audience members who will become spectactors is not a science; it's an art. Still, there are some guidelines that will assist you in the process.

Take your time

Time is your ally. There is no need to rush in the selection of a spectactor. You may feel as though you are on the spot. You are. All the more reason to relax. Your assurance communicates your ability to take care of any spectactor who might share the stage with you.

By taking your time, you may feel as though nothing interesting is happening. From the audience perspective, nothing could be further from the truth. They are watching a process that will result in one of their number being chosen to perform on the stage. That is of the utmost personal interest to everyone. So, again, don't rush.

Consider everybody

To increase your odds of getting a good spectactor to play with, you want as large a pool of candidates as you can get. Remember that there are more people to consider than just those who are sitting in the first few rows.

Beware of volunteers

Say, "I need a volunteer," and you run the risk of winding up with a stage full of extroverts and little kids. True, they are ready to participate, but the quality of their participation may not be ideal. It is better not to ask for a volunteer at all—just select one.

The Perfect Spectactor

You are looking for someone who is self-assured, having a good time, and ready to play, without being hell-bent on proving himself. He would like to participate but doesn't want to appear pushy. If you would just invite him personally, he'd play in a minute. But how can you recognize this person?

Look, Greet, and Listen

When you are looking for potential spectactors, a simple but effective method is to greet people. You are playing a numbers game. Set yourself up to encounter lots of people. As you move among them, look people in the eyes in a friendly way. You are looking for a specific response.

Look for returned eye contact

As you look people in the eyes, watch for the one who is comfortable about returning eye contact and continues to holds your gaze. This is a good sign. Give a nod. If the nod is returned, that is another good sign.

Listen for an assured response

Having established eye contact (and perhaps a nod), now greet this person in a friendly manner. If he returns your greeting, that's a better sign. If he greets you with a strong and assured voice—Jackpot! This is your spectactor.

Considering nominations

When there is a group of people who are all indicating that you should use a particular person from their group, that person is worth your consideration. If the group is pushing someone who obviously does not want to play, forget it. But if the person looks comfortable, or even just hesitant, try the Look/Greet/Listen technique to see what they're like. The nominees to avoid are those who are either absolutely uncomfortable or too cocky.

If at first they say no

When selecting a spectactor, you are walking a fine line between pressure and flexibility. If the person you select refuses, don't immediately look for someone else. If you do, the audience will perceive that it is easy to say no, and it will become twice as difficult to get anyone to participate. Give support and assurance, and use a bit of "peer encouragement" from the audience.

Recouping when they really mean no

If it becomes clear that a person absolutely does not want to participate, never force the issue. Drop it, and quickly turn your attention to someone who has been encouraging the person who said no. The rapid change of focus to a positive person will frequently pick you up a willing spectactor.

More important than the rules

You can follow all of these guidelines and still wind up with a terrible spectactor. (Don't worry. We'll talk about that later.) In the long run, how you select them isn't as important as how you play with them. Within every audience member lies the potential for a great spectactor. Great spectactors are not chosen; they are freed.

Backleading

Backlead. The term comes from ballroom dance.

In the tradition of ballroom dance, the man is supposed to lead and the woman follow. Many men on the dance floor couldn't lead their partner out of a paper bag, but you'd never know it. Why not? Because many women are skilled backleaders. They have mastered the art of appearing to follow the gentleman's lead, which they themselves are, in fact, providing. Some women are so gifted that the men with whom they dance never realize they have been backled.

In interactive work, backleading makes the spectactors feel they are doing a good job of performing. As their confidence increases, so does their creative contribution to the performance. And many spectactors prove to be outstanding actors in their own right.

The purpose of backleading is to free spectactors to contribute to the narrative on their own initiative.

Backleading
Cueing

Cue: to facilitate spectactor participation by giving the spectactor instructions of what to do.

Cueing removes the spectactor's worry about "What am I supposed to do?" Her only responsibility is to pay attention to, and then follow, the instructions.

It is amazing what a spectactor can be cued to do. But look what it can put her through.

> *Run around and cluck like a chicken? No way. I'd look like a fool. I swear, I'm going to kill Chris for getting me up here. I wish I could just leave. But if I walk off the stage now, I'll look like an even bigger fool. Please, God, kill me now. Oh, great. Now the show is stopped, and everyone in the audience is staring at me, waiting for me to cluck like a chicken. Well, if that's the only way I'm going to get off this stage ... "Cluck, cluck, cluck."*

You got her to cluck, but she will probably never come to another interactive show. Cueing produces better long-term results when it does not require the spectactor to do something embarrassing. It may be something as simple as cueing the spectactor to hand an actor a pencil.

There are two ways in which a spectactor can be cued.

Overt cueing

An overt cue is one in which the audience is aware of what the spectactor is expected to do. This can take the form of direct instructions:

"Cut this rope here."

Or the directions may be implied indirectly, as when an actor narrates a story and the spectactor is then expected to enact what has been described.

And Romeo died and fell on the ground ... over there.

Covert cueing

A covert cue consists of instructions given to a spectactor in such a way that the audience is unaware of the cueing. The instructions are given quickly and quietly, when the audience's attention is focused on something else.

There are countless ways to give a covert cue: via written instructions that the audience cannot see; while the spectactor is side-stage, off-stage, or otherwise not in focus; when covered by the noise of audience laughter; as a spectactor is being readied for her performance (put in costume, moved into position, etc.) The key is to communicate information in sneaky and subtle ways. Whatever form is used to give a covert cue, the most important element is that the instructions be brief, simple, and extremely clear.

Cueing and comedy

Cueing is a valuable tool for helping a spectactor to play. Unfortunately, it is frequently used in a way that hinders, rather than helps, a spectactor's creative participation. This happens when cueing is used to create comedy by setting up a spectactor to fail.

> *Here, catch this deck of invisible cards. (He does.) Now, shuffle the cards. (He starts to shuffle the cards.) Wait a minute. You'd better take them out of the case first. (Audience laughs, spectactor feels foolish.)*

The spectactor has just had his worst fears confirmed: If he participates, he will do it wrong and people will laugh. What is worse, he was set up to do it wrong. He may keep playing, but he will be less inclined to initiate anything on his own and more hesitant to follow future instructions, for fear of looking more foolish.

Yes, plenty of people will be good sports about it all; but being a good sport implies that they have lost to begin with. Why get laughs at the expense of the spectactor when it can be generated by her success instead?

Covert cue: "When I lean over, steal the hat from my head."

You lean over, she steals your hat, and the audience goes nuts, because the spectactor apparently got an idea of doing something that "got" you—the mighty performer. The spectactor felt the laughter and applause was for her. Now she is ready to play some more.

The audience love to see one of their own look as good as, or even better than, a performer, and, when they do, they laugh with a different type of laughter. There is no feeling of either superiority or, "Boy, I'm glad that's not me up there." Instead, there is a sense of release and triumph, to see a fellow human being playing without the inhibitions imposed by society, position, and propriety. From this release comes the laughter of freedom.

It is a fulfilling laughter indeed.

Cueing by objective

One risk of cueing is that the spectactors will become nothing more than puppets, waiting for instructions, then doing what they are told. It is a safe way to work, but if you want to be safe, why work with spectactors at all?

You can avoid becoming a puppeteer by telling a spectactor what she wants to accomplish rather than how to accomplish it. Here is an example of a puppet cue:

When I lean across the table, slap my face.

What happens when you lean across the table? She slaps your face. But try cueing her by objective:

When I lean across the table, show that you're not happy with me.

What is she likely to do? Slap your face, walk away from the table, stick out her tongue at you, give you the evil eye, or nothing at all. Who can predict? It's risky, it's on the edge, and it is what makes interactive theatre exciting.

Cueing can be a powerful tool. Use it for the best of what it can do.

Backleading

Endowment

Endow: to relate to a person, object, location, or situation as though it possessed specific qualities or attributes.

As an actor, you already know who your character is, where you are, what is going on, and how you fit in. When spectactors start off, they don't know any of those things. Step inside a spectactor's head for a minute.

> *Oh my god, that actor is talking to me. What am I supposed to do? Am I supposed to pretend that we're really in England? I can't talk with an accent. I don't even know anything about the Renaissance. If I try to say something like an English person, he'll think I'm an idiot. Maybe if I ignore him, he'll go away. I wish he'd leave me alone. I wish I'd gone to Disneyland instead.*

For audience members to become spectactors, they need the tools the interactors have: characters, relationships, objectives, and understanding of the environment. Your job is to endow them with these qualities.

Character — let them know who they are

Always endow your spectactor with a character. Give him a profession, a name, anything to let him know who he is. Otherwise, the spectactor will have no idea who he is "supposed to be" or how he should relate to you. By labeling him, you have given the spectactor a point of reference from which to interact with you.

> *Not Endowed: "Good day. Welcome to the pub."*
>
> *"Uh, thanks."*
>
> *Endowed: "Good day, Captain Sternhelm. Back from the stormy seas to quench your thirst, are you now?"*
>
> *"Uh, yeah. That's right, matey."*

Beware of endowing a spectactor as a character whom you do not recognize at all. It is more reassuring for a spectactor to be endowed with a position, role, or station in life that your character recognizes. This doesn't mean that you have necessarily met him before. It does mean that there is some aspect of his character with which you are familiar. A relationship with a total stranger is not nearly so rich as one with someone you know, or of whom you know.

Character — give them personalities

Even if spectactors know who they are, they won't necessarily know how to behave, so endow them with personalities. Focus on strengths, abilities, and personalities that are fun for them to play.

Be careful when you are endowing a spectactor with negative or lower qualities. One woman may be offended at being endowed as a sexy sleaze-bag, and another may enjoy playing it to the hilt. Endowing requires sensitivity.

It is not so much a question of whether a character is good or bad, nice or mean; it is more whether the character is fun to play. One good guideline is Halloween. Think about what characters people enjoy putting on: pirates, cowboys, monsters, ballerinas, witches, cats. The more fun a spectactor has playing a role, the more he will want to play.

Relationship — give them a trump card

Always endow spectactors in some way that will give them an edge over you. They are smarter, stronger, better looking, more experienced, etc. When spectactors are endowed with a superior quality, they are generally more willing to play.

You can endow something superior even to someone who is below your station or status.

You there, street urchin, come here. I understand that you know many of the goings-on in the back-streets of this city.

Objectives — give them a reason to be here

If a spectactor comes up with something his character wants, great! But why not make it easy for him? Give him an objective to latch onto. Then you can get to playing all the sooner.

"Hey, Eddie, you're right on time. I've got your new carburetor installed. I'll bet you're excited to get racing again."

Give them credit for knowing more than they do

Spectactors don't know as much about the setting, customs, people, laws, etc., as you do. Endow them with having the knowledge. They will relax and play better when they see that you will cover for them on things they don't yet know.

Tell them; don't ask them

Endowing is giving the gift of offers to spectactors. When you ask a question, you are making them come up with the offers themselves.

"From what shire have you come?"

"Uhh . . ."

When they become comfortable and more self-assured, spectactors will generate offers of their own. Until they do, however, it is best not to ask them, but to tell them.

"I understand that you have come from Nottinghamshire. No doubt you encountered thieves."

"Yup. But I escaped."

Spectactor blocking

So you have given a spectactor the wonderful gift of a fabulous character endowment, and what does he do?

"Are you Doctor Lotke?"

"No."   (He blocks.)

The challenge is that you want the spectactor to respond, and the normal way to get a response is to ask a question. But questions usually expect a *yes* or *no* answer (and guess which one the spectactor will chose) or they require the spectactor to invent information.

But there is a way around the dilemma: questions that aren't questions. These are phrases you can use that will endow information without putting it in the form of a question. Yet, if you pause after the statement, it is clear to the spectactor that he is expected to respond.

> *I have heard that . . .*
> *I understand that . . .*
> *So this is your . . .*
> *No doubt you are . . .*
> *And this must be . . .*
> *And you would be . . .*

First and finally—throw an assumption

Stuck for an endowment? Throw an assumption—any assumption. That's the basis for endowing. You owe him money. You spilled wine on her gown last month. They are bringing you news from your brother. Make an assumption!

Backleading
Blind Offers

Blind Offer: an offer that is made unconsciously, without the intent of communicating information.

If all you do is endow spectactors, they are being passively creative. The next step is to make them actively creative. How do you do this when they don't know what to do? What if they are not doing anything?

Look again. They are making blind offers. He is standing with his weight on one hip. She is scratching her arm. They both giggled when you looked at them. Your job is to transform blind offers made by audience members into defined offers made by characters within the plot of the story.

A spectactor sits down. (That is a blind offer.)

You sit down beside him and say, "Oh man, my feet are killing me, too. If Mister McClusky makes us climb that wall one more time, I say we ditch out behind the gym."

By transforming his blind offer into a defined offer you have accomplished two things: You have made the spectactor feel that he has done something right, even though he didn't intend to "do" anything at all. You have also made what he did a part of the story. He starts to feel as though he is performing. His next offer stands a good chance of being defined rather than blind.

Backleading
Steps

Step: an increment of "room" which is provided so that a spectactor may fill it with his or her own offer.

> *Baby is just learning to walk. She is standing next to a chair, hanging on for balance (and for dear life). You are standing on the far side of the room. "Come on. You can do it. Walk to me. Whoo dat widdo babykins wookin' at me? Come on . . ." While your baby-talk may be very persuasive, she's not budging an inch. So you go stand right next to the chair, hold out your hands just barely beyond her reach, and she does it! One giant step for baby, and she has reached you. You praise and praise that single step, re-attach her to the chair, and back up two steps away. And before you know it, that baby's walking all over the darn place without any help from you.*

When you create the first step, you are establishing a supportive situation in which a spectactor can feel safe making a small offer. Each step that follows encourages the spectactor to make progressively bigger offers. And before you know it, that spectactor is playing all over the darn place, without any help from you.

Start with the physical

It is far easier for spectactors to begin with physical tasks. That is because they perceive a physical task as being more within their realm of capability than coming up with something to say. Spectactors feel less on the spot when they have been given a simple task to accomplish.

Start small to build big

Don't ask spectactors to step too far outside their comfort zones at first. If you want him to run, start by getting him to walk quickly, jog, trot, and then run.

Use the buddy system

When backleading spectactors to do something challenging, you set them more at ease if you do it with them. The spectactor who won't yell alone may be willing to yell along with you.

Use momentum

Momentum can also help a spectactor take a big step. Here's how: Build the momentum of what is going on until it is really rolling; then draw the spectactor into the action without giving her time to stop and think. It's like running and jumping into a cold pool instead of going in one foot at a time.

Expect a lot from them

Small steps don't mean small expectations. A little hole in a dam will eventually give way to the stored-up power of the water.

Inside of everyone is stored the ability to play. It's not always evident, because some folks are scared of it, others are out of practice, and an unfortunate few have forgotten how.

When you offer steps to spectactors, you are giving them the opportunity to remember that they know how to play. As their assurance builds, the power of their playful spirit is released. Then, watch out!

Backleading
Primers

Now that you know how to ease a spectactor into playing, here are some formats that will make that process even quicker.

It is like priming their creative pumps: You still have to work like the devil at first, but the good stuff shows up a lot quicker.

View and resolve

People are more comfortable playing after seeing a bit of the scene they are going into, so begin by playing out a conflict between actors without involving the spectactors. This allows them to observe and get important information relevant to the issue. Then notice the spectactors, and endow them with a reason that their characters are able to resolve the conflict.

Tell me about it

Start by setting forth the information that you want the spectactor to run with. Invent the set-up for her. Then get her to expand on the story by asking her to to tell you about it.

So you baked three thousand gingerbread
cookies all by yourself and gave them to your
sister for a special occasion? Tell me about
that.

The tricky business of using questions

Risky questions

When you first begin speaking to spectactors, avoid questions that can be answered by
a simple *yes* or *no*. Spectactors will frequently
opt for *no*, which blocks your offer.

> *"Did you go by the graveyard at night?"*
>
> *"No."*

Even if they opt for *yes*, it can still be a dead-
end street, because there is that big, gaping hole
in the dialogue following the *yes* response.

> *Actor: "Did you go by the graveyard at night?"*
> *Spectactor: "Yes."*
> *Pause.*
> *Actor: "That's nice."*

A skilled interactor should be able to do better than "That's nice," but it's a whole lot easier if
you can backlead the spectactor into a response
more stimulating than a simple "yes." After the
spectactor has played with you a bit, *yes/no*

questions can be a natural part of the conversation. But when you're first starting out, they can be a problem.

Another risky type of question to avoid when starting out is an open-ended question— one to which the answer could be almost anything.

"Where did you go last night?"

"Uuuhhh."

The spectactor thinks there is a right answer and he doesn't know what it is. So he hesitates, for fear of saying the wrong thing.

Multiple choice questions.

An effective primer that makes it easy for a spectactor to play is a multiple choice question. He doesn't have to invent anything at all. All he has to do is choose one of the options you give him. If he doesn't pick any of your options, but makes up another answer, that's even better! He didn't block you; he just initiated a new offer of his own.

"When you went by the graveyard, was it last Thursday or Friday night?"

"It was Saturday."

"Midnight on Saturday night! You must have nerves of steel."

Potent Questions

A potent question is one that will lead easily to a full answer from a spectator. It introduces the topic and can be answered without specialized knowledge.

How did you manage to catch those three horses that got loose from your barn?

Fill in the blank

When you are endowing a spectactor, leave space in your conversation that she can fill in with her own offer. If she doesn't say anything, you can give her clues that will help her to fill in the blank.

"So he was reading that lovely sonnet that he wrote for you. The one called . . ."

(You pause, as though trying to remember, giving the spectactor a chance to fill in the title. But she says nothing.)

". . . the one called 'The Little . . .'" (You pause again, but still nothing.) "It was some kind of a river . . ."

"Brook?"

"That's it. 'The Little Brook.'"

Connect the dots

You can set up a spectactor to look brilliant by playing connect the dots. Offer two independent pieces of information between which you see an obvious connection. Leave room for the spectactor to point out the connection. If it eludes her, gradually make it more obvious, until she discovers the connection herself. When applied to humor, this technique is like setting up the straight-lines of a joke and then helping the spectactor come up with the punchline.

> *"That's peculiar. Maria just asked to borrow my hat pin, and that silly voodoo priestess doesn't even wear a hat." (clutches stomach) "Ow. Must be something I ate."*
>
> *"Maybe she's doing voodoo on you."*
>
> *"My heavens, you may be right!"*

Get them to help you.

People like to feel useful. If you can put the spectactors to work doing something with you or for you—do it. In this way they can participate and remain relatively un-self-conscious, because their attention is focused on completing their task.

Actor Failure Syndrome

An actor performs a task successfully for a little while, then suddenly fails. When a spect-actor lends a hand to help the actor out, she is given the new position of responsibility for the task. This gives the spectactor position, status, and an objective, out of which the scene can continue.

> *Mr. Weller (the actor) has been dazzling the audience with his skill as a rhyming toastmaster. He is offered yet another first line to turn into a rhyming toast.*
>
> *"Here's to loved ones far and wide . . .*
> *May God grant them to . . . to be . . ."*
>
> *Sam appears to be stumped. An audience member tries to help him out. "By our side."*
>
> *"Good! We have a new rhyming toastmaster!"*

Everyone applauds the new spectactor and she is given the position of honor to offer the next rhyming toast.

Title topics

When a spectactor has made an offer, link it to a title topic that is open to a variety of interpreta-tions. The topic gives the spectactor a framework within which to take his offer wherever he likes.

"I met my wife on the ship."

"On the ship? So that's how you became involved in 'The Great Licorice Caper.'"

"Yes, she liked licorice all right. But, then, so did the Count."

Gossip

For some reason, many spectactors are comfortable gossiping. Perhaps because gossip is frequently inaccurate, so there is no right or wrong. Perhaps because they've had a lot of practice. Whatever the reason, it is an easy way to get people to play.

"I've heard that Colonel Balderdash has a history with a certain young blond woman. As I remember, your maid used to work for the Colonel. What does she say?"

"Well, I really shouldn't tell, but she did mention that the Colonel has been seeing that peroxide minx on the fly for two years now."

Gossip makes a good primer, because you can use it to lead a spectactor into action. When you link an offer from his gossip to a plot element or another character, it is not unusual for the spectactor to want to pursue the issue further, and thus initiate action.

Backleading a pre-written scene

Backleading can lead to more than just gossip, interviews, and storytelling. You can do it in scene work, too. It is possible to play a scene with a spectactor in which there are dialogue and blocking, just as you would do a scripted and directed scene with another performer.

First, you need to know all the lines and blocking for both characters, yours and the spectactor's. You begin by performing your lines and blocking. Leave space for the spectactor to say her lines. If nothing happens, start backleading. You know what she should have said; get her to say it, or find a way for your character to say it for her. Be ready to encourage and build on any offer she makes. If you need to, you can bend it to bring her offer back on line with the intent of the script.

Backleading a script is quite a zen experience. You have to hold tight to what should happen and let go for what does happen, all at the same time.

Secret objective

Another way to get spectactors active is to play secret objective with them. This forces you to be defined in your backleading.

First, you must know what you want the spectator to do. Then you start feeding him clues, so that eventually he will recognize what he is expected to do and then do it. The beauty of secret objective is that even if the spectactor doesn't figure out what he is supposed to do, the interchange still makes an interesting scene.

Routines

As hazardous as an unbroken routine can be to good narrative, it can be an incredibly beneficial primer for audience participation.

What makes a routine such an effective primer is its recognition value. The spectator is already familiar with the routine, so she is comfortable participating, because she knows what is supposed to happen, what to say, and how to behave.

What routines make good primers? Wedding ceremonies, picnics, job interviews, doing dishes, washing the car, shopping for presents, cliff diving in Acapulco, et cetera, et cetera, et cetera.

Play off spectator expertise

A spectactor will play better if he feels competent to meet the task at hand.

Hand a plumber a pair of scissors and say, "Miss Boggs needs a wash, rinse, cut, and perm," and you're likely to get a laugh and a look of, "What am I supposed to do now?" But hand him a wrench and say, "The left-hand sink just won't stop dripping," and you're likely to have that sink fixed in no time.

This doesn't mean that plumbers can play only plumbers, but it is a great primer to play into something they know—baseball, needlepoint, sailing, comic books, old war stories—you name it.

Play on universal themes

This is another example of using something that people know. There are themes that span the continents and the ages: the battle of the sexes, the quest for riches, the loss of a single sock in the wash. Involve spectactors in a universal theme, and once again they have familiar ground on which to play.

Backleading
Strokes

Stroke: to give positive reinforcement to a spect-actor for his or her offer.

You have worked your fingers to the bone, trying to get a spectactor to play. You've endowed, you've transformed blind offers, you've used a primer. And suddenly the unthinkable happens: the spectactor makes an offer all on his own. What do you do now?

Stroke, stroke, stroke.

The instant that a spectactor makes a defined offer or a build, give him a stroke. It doesn't matter how small a step it is; if he has taken a step, STROKE!

"And on the pond, you caught a fish."

"Uh huh. A bass."

"My gosh! The Bass of Duncton Pond! That fish has eluded the best fishermen of this county for years. You must be a darned good fisherman."

Strokes build the confidence of a spectactor. When he musters up his courage to take a little creative step, and is immediately rewarded for his efforts, he is likely to take an even bigger step the next time. And when that next time comes around, he will have even more information to play with, because a good stroke also contains a build.

Best of all, a stroke strengthens that most fragile of creatures—self-esteem. For many spect-actors, the line between who they are personally and the characters they are playing is blurry at best. Strokes reinforce the self-image of spect-actors. And as their personal sense of assurance increases, the spectactors become more fearless in playing their characters.

Don't patronize

Be careful not to let your strokes become patronizing. No one likes to be treated like a child, not even little children. The best way to avoid this pitfall is to make each stroke an honestly respectful reward for a spectactor's creative contribution.

Incorporation

So now you have done a masterful job of backleading. You have turned a group of nervous, unsure audience members into an insatiable pack of spectactors. What are you supposed to do now?

What do you do when every offer you make is blocked by one of theirs? What do you do when they're making great offers that weren't a part of the original story? What do you do when their work is full of anachronisms? What do you do once they've caught the bug and are playing full speed ahead without any help from you?

Relax. It's time to incorporate.

Incorporation
Bending

Bend: to accept and redirect an offer through justification.

The first rule of incorporation is this: Everything the spectactor does is right. No exceptions. Making an audience offer fit within the narrative is the responsibility of the interactor, not the spectactor.

No matter how far off the mark the spectactor's offer is, never block it. Blocking the offer tells the spectactor, "You're wrong." Tell spectactors they are wrong, and they will start to play against you, or they'll stop playing altogether.

So what are you supposed to do? Go along with whatever they say or do? Yes. And no.

Don't block — Bend

First, go along with the offer, no matter how inappropriate it may be. Always begin by accepting the offer.

Second, don't go along blindly. If there is a need to modify the offer, you can do so at the very same time that you are accepting it. That's a bend.

Bending can get you into or out of most any situation. It allows you to accomplish practically any objective. Here are some common uses for the bend:

- Dealing with anachronisms
- Putting a spectactor on track
- Converting spectactor blocks into offers

Transforming anachronisms

Dealing with anachronisms is a common use of the bend. You will find a section later on in this book devoted exclusively to handling anachronisms. For now, just remember: Bend; don't block.

Putting spectactors on track

Sometimes spectactors focus on tangents that will not be fulfilled in the narrative. Sometimes they don't know what to focus on at all. You can put them on track, without ever letting them feel that they were off the track, by bending their offer.

"We think Mister Dunbar has a boat."

(The boat has nothing to do with the plot. They need to focus on the fact that Mister Dunbar is near-sighted.)

*"Yes, he does. Of course, he never uses it any
more, not with his bad vision and all."*

Converting spectactor blocks to offers

Bending can give a spectactor a second
chance to play, by turning his block into an offer.

"What do you say we head over to the pub?"

"I'm not thirsty."

*"Grabbed a quick pint before I got here, eh?
Serves me right for being late."*

The four-step bend
Accept - Justify - Stroke - Link

(The setting is the sixteenth century.)

Spectactor: "Look at that plane up there."

*Actor: (Accept) "Indeed!" (Justify) "Such a
plain hawk to be found in such a glorious time
as ours." (Stroke) "Thou hast most keen eyes."
(Link) "Pray, cast them upon this ring and tell
me if its stone be true, for I have paid most
dearly for it."*

Accepting makes the spectactor feel that you are not at odds with him. Justifying brings his offer into line with the narrative. Stroking identifies a positive quality about the spectactor. And linking directs that positive quality to something within the narrative.

The two-step bend
Accept - Justify

Not every bend requires four steps. Sometimes accepting and justifying will do the job just fine. Whenever possible, follow a two-step bend with a new offer.

> *A little kid: "You're not real."*
>
> *Actor: "You're right. I haven't felt like myself at all lately. Let's go to the park. Then I'll feel better."*

Use it, but don't abuse it

A final word of caution: Don't bend unless it is essential. If spectactors feel that everything they say or do will be twisted to another purpose, they may stop making offers.

Remember, your objective is to get spectactors to introduce new and unexpected elements to the narrative. Never bend an offer simply because you have a "better idea" in mind.

Incorporation
Weaving

Weave: to integrate spectactors and their offers into the existing plot in such a way that both become essential to the story.

Now it's time for the real magic. When spectactors start making their own offers, that's good. When those offers are woven into the existing plot and become essential to the story, that's magic. That's interactive theatre.

How do you make the magic happen? Focus on making their offers become primary story elements within the narrative. Involve spectactors in ways that make them featured characters within the established plot.

Here are some weaving techniques:

Go with their offer

If you don't pick up a spectactor's offer, you have nothing to weave. Give high priority to the development of offers made by spectactors. (Remember, you can use both blind offers and intentional offers.) See where the offers will lead you. As you are building and developing a spectactor's offer, the way to weave it into the story will often become apparent.

Link their offers to major plot elements

When a spectactor makes an offer, find a way in which it can become essential to the development of the narrative.

> *Main narrative: Fast Eddie is trying to pull the con of the century.*
>
> *Spectactor offer: "I am a writer."*
>
> *Link to main plot: Fast Eddie thinks that a newspaper article on his philanthropy would reassure his intended mark. Perhaps the "writer" would be willing to write such an article in exchange for a cut of the take.*

Hand-offs

When you are nearing the end of an encounter with spectactors, look for a reason to hand them off to another character, based on what has evolved out of your interchange with them. Create a link that will give them a motivation to meet and interact with another performer.

Hooks and pay-offs

This is one of the real "magic tricks" of interactive theatre. A spectactor does something, says something, or has something that clearly could not have been anticipated in the original narrative.

Later in the story, that unanticipated element becomes a crucial part of the story, just as if it had been in the script all along. It's a two-step process.

Find a hook: Listen carefully for spectactor offers that are not in the original story, or look for a personal possession, skill, or attribute unique to the spectactor. This becomes your "hook." If the hook is an object, skill, or attribute, make a mental note of it, but say nothing. If the hook is an offer, then accept, do a build, and let it go.

Reincorporate and pay-off: Don't spot the hook and immediately jump to the pay-off. The audience will spot the connection. Let a significant amount of time pass, then reincorporate. It will seem magical, because the earlier appearance of the hook will have been forgotten by many in the audience.

When the time is right, create a scenario that builds to a point in which the hook becomes essential to the resolution of the scene. Don't offer the solution of the hook yourself; let the offer come from the spectactor. If the offer doesn't come, do a little backleading.

Object hook:
You note that a spectactor has a penknife on his keychain. Later in the day, you see the spectactor

nearby. You create a scenario in which the bark from a spice stick must be shaved off to make a medicinal tea for a sick child. You have no blade fine enough to do the job. If only there were someone with such a blade, the child's life might be saved. You make sure the spectactor sees the scene. If he takes the initiative—oh glorious day— he has saved the child's life. If he does nothing, you skillfully back-lead the audience until he (or someone else) brings forth a knife, and, oh glorious day . . .

Skill hook:

You learn that a spectactor can juggle. Later on, you establish a scenario with a fellow interactor in which you boast that you possess special powers through which you can make balls juggle in the air without touching them. Your fellow inter-actor puts you to the test by making a sizable wager that you cannot. You accept the wager, then begin by getting your betting partner to acknowledge that your "target" spectactor's body is in no way your own. You win the bet and achieve the pay-off when you use your special powers of persuasion to convince the spectactor to pick up the balls and juggle.

Attribute hook:

You notice a small tattoo of a rose on a woman's shoulder. Later, you create a scenario in which she and her friends overhear you describing the loss of your sister at sea many years ago, a sister whom a rogue Spaniard marked with the sign of the rose when she was but a very young child. Mention the "sign of the rose upon her shoulder" clearly enough, and soon you are likely to find yourself having a joyful reunion that is initiated by your long-lost sister.

Offer hook:

A spectactor has earlier offered that one of his horses was recently stolen. You set up a scenario in which a horse thief is captured and convicted, based on the testimony of the spectactor.

Beyond participation

Weaving transforms the experience of participation into one of empowerment. When spectactors' contributions are truly integrated, the entire story becomes more personally meaningful, because they have shared the responsibility for its creation.

Rough Edges

Interactive theater is full of rough edges. All sorts of variables come into play when audience members become spectactors. But unlike the rough edges in many fields of endeavor, rough edges are a part of the appeal of interactive performances.

Rough edges become both the price and the evidence of a form that celebrates the here and now and the unpredictable relationships between human beings involved in the creative process.

Fine acting and a mastery of defined improvisational techniques are essential to good interactive performance; but when the audience is permitted—encouraged—to impact the content and the direction of the show, and when audience members assume significant roles within the show, those facts introduce an element of uncertainty, of not knowing what will come next, that makes interactive theatre exciting. There is a certain thrill in watching performers successfully deal with difficult, unexpected, and unpredictable situations.

The techniques addressed in this section won't eliminate the rough edges; they will give you the ability to recognize them and deal effectively with them. For they are a unique part of the fabric of interactive theatre.

Rough Edges
Anachronisms

Anachronism: any offer that violates the reality of the established premise.

The dictionary defines an anachronism as something that is chronologically out of place; e.g., a pay-phone in the Middle Ages. In interactive theatre, an anachronism also includes anything that violates the reality of the premise; e.g., a pay-phone in a submarine.

Any time you are creating the illusion of reality, anachronisms will abound, whether as inappropriate objects physically present or as inappropriate information given in the form of offers.

But fear not, there are things you can do to defuse the anachronisms that threaten to undermine that ever so fragile reality you have struggled to create.

Anachronistic humor

If the audience needs to refer to something outside the premise to understand a joke, that's anachronistic humor. Amazingly, interactors (who work very hard to create a believable illusion) will undermine their own premise with anachronistic humor, even more frequently than spectactors do.

> *The premise is fifteenth-century England. You approach a local peasant (spectactor) and ask, "What thinkest thou of our beloved Sir Francis Drake?" You then hold a turkey drumstick out like a microphone for the peasant's answer. Everyone laughs. (True, you never called your drumstick a microphone, but the laugh came because the audience recognized it as such.)*

The appeal of anachronistic humor is that it gets easy laughs. If you are concerned only with getting laughs, it works. If you want to maintain the integrity of the story, if you want the audience to play within the context of the location and period, don't use it.

Anachronistic humor sends mixed signals to the audience. On the one hand, you are asking them to *pretend,* as though the premise were real, while, on the other hand, your joke makes a point of the fact that it is not. If you play anachronistically, you can be sure the spectactors will play that way as well.

Does this mean no jokes? Absolutely not. There is plenty of humor to be found within the reality of a premise. It is richer humor because it is integral to the whole. And if you are concerned with being a hot-shot in regard to your comic skills, it demonstrates a great deal more skill when you can get a laugh within the context of a premise.

The question becomes: Are you working to create a narrative or are you interested only in getting laughs?

Ignorable anachronisms

So if you are avoiding anachronisms, what do you do about the ones the spectactors introduce? (For they *will* introduce them.)

Some anachronisms can be ignored: a person wearing a Mickey Mouse t-shirt in Nazi Germany, a drinking fountain in Elizabethan England, Ancient Greeks speaking in modern English. If the spectactors don't point out anachronisms, neither should you. You are creating an illusion, not reality. The fact of the matter is that nothing fits in the period. You're pretending. If no one else notices, you don't need to either.

Some performers take pride in pointing out anachronisms, to show how "real" they are and how much they know about the period.

(Pirate looking at a camera) "What is that strange device you hold in your hand? I have

never seen such a thing. Perhaps it is a hand cannon, or a soul-snatcher."

Pointing out something that is obviously out of place only diminishes whatever illusion of reality has been created. It keeps spectactors from pretending in the period, because they are yanked back to the present.

Once again, don't block — bend

If a spectactor brings up an anachronism, it becomes something to deal with. First rule of thumb: Don't block it; bend it. You are helping the spectator by transforming his anachronism into an appropriate offer. It also helps ease him into playing within the established premise. Audiences are very impressed by the ability to transmute anachronisms into useful offers. Here are some techniques for doing so:

Translate

You can bend an anachronistic offer by translating it into something that fits within the premise.

"I'll put it on my credit card."

"Most well, good sir. A letter of credit will be entirely satisfactory from one of your high station."

Use faulty hearing

What your character hears does not always have to be exactly what a spectactor has said. (Grandparents have been demonstrating this for ages.)

"Fax him this letter."

"Yes, all the facts seem to be accurate. I'll send it to the general by Pony Express immediately."

If it becomes a debate, politely walk away

If a spectactor is determined not to let you bend an anachronism, go play with someone else. You won't win a debate.

Anachronistic questions

There always seem to be people who want to talk about something outside the reality of the premise: "What is the quickest way to the freeway from here? Who made these costumes? Do you really get paid to do this?"

You can't ignore them, you shouldn't block them, and you don't want to break the premise. What's an interactor to do?

Try staying in character and bending the question so that it becomes relevant to the premise.

"Are you a college student?"

"If only I were. Here on the island of Tuki-Tuki, only the very rich can afford to attend the university."

Oh, that's right. You guys have to stay in character all the time. I could never do that."

Sometimes spectactors think you just didn't understand, so they try again.

"No, I mean, really. Do you go to college in the area?"

"I would love to. Do you know someone who could get me in?"

If they are persistent, don't keep bending; it will only frustrate them. Refer them to another source for the information they are seeking: the program, the ushers, box office personnel, etc.

"I can't believe this. All I want is a simple answer. Do you go to college or not?"

"If you speak to the people where you came in, I'm sure they can give you the information you are seeking."

Spectacting

A spectactor is not usually a trained performer. He may not know his upstage from his downstage. Ask her to speak from her diaphragm, and you may get a very puzzled look. It is your responsibility to help them perform successfully.

A spectactor may be doing a great job of playing a character and making fabulous offers, but if the audience can't easily see or hear him, it is all for naught. Here are some ways to help.

Spectactors who upstage themselves

When performing, many spectactors face the actor to whom they are speaking and, as a result, they turn away from the audience. When a spectactor has thus upstaged himself, the audience cannot see his face and frequently cannot hear what he is saying.

It is the interactor's responsibility to be sure that the spectactor is facing out. This may involve physically turning the spectactor so that he is open to the audience. It may also be accomplished by the interactor upstaging himself while the spectactor is in focus, then "cheating out" when he needs focus.

Setting an example by addressing both the audience and the spectactor will sometimes encourage the spectactor to do the same.

The spectactor should never feel as though she is being herded around the stage or molded into position. Always find some justification for the way you get her to face out.

Speaking too quietly

Spectactors frequently cannot be heard. Many have never had to project their voice to a large group. Using a microphone is not always possible, or even desirable. There are at least two other ways to make sure that the audience hears what the spectactor has said.

The first is for the interactor to communicate the information the spectactor has just offered, without sounding as though he is just repeating the line.

> *"The thing that first attracted you to your husband was his . . ."*
>
> *(quietly) "Good looks."*
>
> *"Yes, indeed, that tight little butt of his. He's one fine looking man."*

Another alternative is to position yourself some distance away from the spectactor. The need to speak to someone farther away causes most spectactors to speak in a voice that can be heard by the rest of the audience as well.

Rough Edges
Bad Spectactors

There is no such thing as a bad spectactor, just as there is no such thing as a bad audience. In both cases, it's just a matter of how much time you are willing to invest in creating a rapport that works. There are times when the spectactor is just not working out, and no matter what you do, it only gets worse. Here are some "rules of thumb" for what to do then.

The basic guideline is this: If the spectactor's work is going to blemish the show, let it ride; if it is going to damage the show, it is time to take action.

Always push beyond the easy limits. Sometimes you have to be willing to drown a little before the spectactor begins to swim.

But don't unnecessarily prolong the audience's agony. If it is time to take action, remove the character, recast the role, or rewrite the show. Let your creativity, your sensitivity, and your intuition be your guides.

What you must do, do quickly—and with a light touch.

Rough Edges
Obnoxious Audience

He's drunk and thinks he's more interesting than the show.

She's out to show what big breasts she has.

He has confused heckling with participating.

She's screaming because someone stepped on her little girl's foot.

Sometimes there are audience members who become a major disruption during an interactive performance. Frequently, they are not spectactors at all, but members of the viewing audience. Their participation is ruining the show for the rest of the audience. These are the Obnoxious Audience—OA's. What do you do with an OA?

Don't fight them

If you become an OA's adversary, you are only adding fuel to the fire. You are perpetuating his obnoxiousness by giving him someone to fight. If you don't allow yourself to become his opponent, he won't be able to fight. You can't chase a person who won't run.

Never lose your cool

If you lose your cool, you also lose your power in the situation. The OA knows it. What's worse, everyone else knows it, too. Don't let an OA turn you into an obnoxious interactor.

Ignore hecklers

No matter how snappy a comeback you can deliver, you are not going to improve the situation by responding to a heckler.

Stand-up comics shoot down hecklers all the time, sometimes as part of the act, sometimes for survival. But stand-ups are more concerned with playing *for* the audience than *with* them.

The business of interactive theatre is getting the audience to become creative and cooperative players. You aren't going to create a great sense of trust by nailing a heckler to the back wall with a brilliant improvisational put-down.

The heckler heckles because he wants attention. If you respond in any way at all (a comment to him or about him, or even just a look) he is getting what he wants. The best way to deal with a heckler is to ignore him completely. This gets difficult when he keeps on heckling, but that is when it is most important to remain oblivious to him, because that is about the time that the audience will side with the performers and silence the heckler through peer pressure.

And if the heckling continues, there's always Higher Authority.

Make the ringleader your ally

Many times, a group of OA's will have a ringleader. Take the ringleader aside to allow her to save face. When you have her away from the group, treat her as though she is on your side. If you put her in charge of seeing that her group behaves appropriately, the ringleader will often behave appropriately as well.

> *"I can see that you and your friends are having a good time at my cafe. I'm so glad. Perhaps you could see that your friends enjoy themselves a little more quietly. It is a bit distracting to the other guests. And of course you know how easily distracted they can be. I appreciate your help. I knew I could depend on you."*

Another actor takes the spectactor's side

Sometimes, when an audience member is angry with something that a character has done, the

OA's anger can be defused by another character who takes her side.

"He stepped on my little girl's toe!"

"My god! He is such the clumsy oaf. I'm going to have to have a word with him about this."

Drunks

If an OA is not too drunk, try to make him your ally. If he is beyond hope, leave him to the Higher Authority.

Higher Authority

There should always be someone in a position of higher authority to turn to as a last resort. That person should not be an actor, but someone whom the OA will perceive as being "outside the show," with the authority to do whatever it takes to keep the experience pleasant for the rest of the audience. The person of higher authority must possess the velvet skill of a diplomat and the iron control of a bouncer.

Rough Edges

Caustic Characters

Some people are evil, conniving, two-faced, depraved, vicious, immoral, and a blot on the human race. And actors love to play them. But new challenges occur when a caustic character steps beyond the fourth wall and into direct contact with spectactors.

People love to hate a villain

Some spectactors enjoy playing with caustic characters. They eat it up when the mean, nasty sheriff spews his venomous wrath upon them. There is a certain satisfaction in seeing someone behave despicably and get away with it. There is also a dark pleasure in seeing one's friends become the object of a characters disdain. And when someone is mean and nasty, it gives you license to retaliate with your own attack.

But mean and nasty has its problems.

The hazards of caustic combat

The first problem with putting people in the attack/retaliation mode is that it is frequently too easy for them slip into it. It's a sad comment on human nature, but many people are more comfortable attacking and retaliating than they are being playful and vulnerable. It doesn't take much for venom spewing, put-downs, sarcasm, rudeness, and the like to become the point of the interaction. And that gets old very quickly.

Another problem is that spectactors get conditioned to respond this way. Such a response may be fine while they are playing with the mean and nasty sheriff, but it presents difficulties when they start relating in the same way to the sweet, befuddled seamstress.

The final thing to consider is that there are many people who don't enjoy attacking and retaliating, even if it's all in good fun. When these people see how others are treated, they will no longer be interested in playing as spectactors themselves.

Caustic without compromise

So what are you supposed to do when you are playing with spectactors and you don't want to violate your caustic character by becoming a sweet little goody-two-shoes?

First, remember that you can direct your obnoxious nature at people who are not present in the scene. Pick on the radio commentator who appeared in the show three scenes prior to the present one. Focus your venom on the school teacher from an earlier scene. But what do you do if the spectactors you have berated come into the scene again at a later time? Why not treat them politely? Being a two-faced back-stabber is certainly in keeping with a caustic nature.

Give spectactors the edge

There are times when it is essential for you to inflict your caustic nature directly upon a spectactor. In those cases you have two jobs to do: attack, and give them the edge.

The edge is anything that gives the spect-actor a way to get a win in the exchange. It may be a flaw in logic that allows her to win an argument, an obvious foible that allows him to put you in your place, or even an opening that allows her to do something behind your back after your character has apparently won.

The best edge that spectactors can have occurs when another interactor takes their side. They now have someone to stand beside them, to look out for their interests, and to support their self-esteem.

That is also to your advantage, because it provides you a player who knows the battle at hand is a cooperative venture. You now have the option to focus your attack on your fellow actor's character, and the freedom to leave that character decimated, without concern that anyone will take it personally.

The audience still has someone to root for, someone to defend, someone with whom to empathize; but now, that person (the actor) is someone who knows how to make the caustic exchange serve the narrative rather than letting it degenerate into a battle of nastiness for its own sake.

Don't break the trust

One final warning: It takes a great deal of trust for an interactor to suffer the slings and arrows of a caustic character. More so than in traditional theatre. In traditional theatre, actors say lines that have already been written; they have no choice in the matter. But interactors are often improvising lines, so the question can arise: "Is he playing his character, or is he really being mean to me?"

If you let a caustic character become a weapon with which you attack actors and spectactors, rather than the characters they are playing, you destroy the trust that is essential to interactive work. And it's all downhill from there.

Interactoring

A lot of interactive technique is focused on facilitating spectactors' work. But there is one person's work you should make sure doesn't get lost in the shuffle—your own.

In addition to helping the spectactors create memorable performances, you are still responsible for giving a great performance of your own. Audiences want to be moved, engaged, enlightened, and transported by your work as well.

That's just a matter of being a good actor and improvisor, right?

Not quite.

In interactive shows, acting and improvising bring with them their own hidden traps and opportunities. This section will help you avoid the traps and seize the opportunities, as they appear within your own work as an interactor.

Interactoring
Lead and Fill

Much of straight improvisation is played as a true ensemble, with everyone contributing something to the direction of the story. The ensemble method leads to rich and varied results and has tremendous value. But recognizing the value of the "group mind" should not be reason to ignore the potential of the individual to lead as well.

Lead and fill in music

Take another look at jazz music. Sometimes the combo is playing as an ensemble. But then they come to the sax break. The drummer, bass player, and pianist ease back and play fill, and the sax player takes lead. That doesn't mean the rest of the players aren't contributing. The bass player is laying down the bass line, the drummer holds the tempo solid, the pianist keeps the chord progression going; and, of course, each one is still free to add a little spice every now and then. But there is no question that for the next sixteen bars the sax player is the one leading the direction of the musical exploration.

So how does this apply to interactive work?

Theatrical lead and fill

Whether you are improvising with other performers or interacting with spectactors, there are times where it is useful to have one player take lead while the others play fill. The point is not to be proprietary about the story development, but to allow a single vision to move it forward for a period of time. This is not a better way to create narrative, just a different way.

Lead and fill can help avoid feeding frenzies. Sometimes a performer will discover a spectactor who is very willing to play. Suddenly, the spectactor is besieged with interactors, each trying to backlead the poor soul in a different direction. Playing lead and fill allows the interaction to take a focused direction with the support of those playing fill.

Another use of lead and fill is to make it easy for a group to know when it is time to move on to the next plot point. When the person playing lead moves on, all the other players are ready to go, too.

Playing lead

Playing lead is not like playing *the* lead. Any character, even a minor one, can do it. When someone "plays lead," it means only that that person is responsible for introducing the primary offers that will guide the progression and direction of the story.

Playing fill

When playing fill, it is your job to support the directions in which the story is being led. You maintain what has been established by keeping the characters, environment, and objectives alive and real. And you don't make offers that are going to drastically redirect the narrative.

Does it all seem pretty uncreative? Think of it like a coloring book. The lines have been drawn for you, but what a difference in the picture before and after the crayons have done their thing.

How to know who's who

How do you identify who is lead and who is fill? The methods are as unlimited as your imagination will allow. You can set up who will play lead ahead of time. Lead can be the first person to start working with the spectactor. You can even use hand signals to indicate who is taking lead.

How to switch between lead and fill

You can define the switch by time (e.g., five minutes as lead, then switch). You can do it by narrative (e.g., one person plays lead until a specific plot point is reached). Or you can hand off lead and fill during a scene with signals that the audience is unaware of. Here again, your imagination is the only limit.

The hazard of lead and fill

The down-side of lead and fill occurs when it is done for personal gain. That happens when an improvisor takes over and starts "driving" the scene. It is done not out of cooperation, but out of a desire to control.

Effective use of lead and fill requires the support and cooperation of all the performers. Then it is not a method of controlling the story at the expense of the ensemble. Instead, it becomes another tool to make the process of creating narrative effective, varied, and interesting.

Interactoring
Character

Character is essential in most any type of acting. The techniques used to create a clearly defined interactive character should be familiar, because they are used in traditional acting work as well. But while the basis is the same, in interactive theatre the application is a little different. Here are some tips that will make your character more effective in an interactive setting.

Make your character easily identifiable

Interactive character work is not always as subtle as traditional theatre, and for good reason. In interactive theatre there are elements that tend to distract the audience: the proximity of the performers, an unfamiliar performance style; the audience's own sense of self-consciousness. Your character must be clear and recognizable, because your identity must be able to cut through the distractions.

Use names

The most common way to recognize a character is by name. People need to hear a name more than once to be able to remember it later in the show. Find ways to bring your name into the conversation several times when the audience first meets your character. The use of names is especially important when you are talking directly to spectactors. You can also ease the strain of the name game by using other characters' names when they are first introduced.

Don't take this business of names to the point of ridiculousness, but use them frequently enough to let the audience know who people are. After a while, you can ease back, and they will have the first step to identity—the characters' names.

Get a job

What do you do for a living? How long have you been doing it? What is your position? Do you have a title? These are other familiar identifiers, that help an audience get a handle on your character.

Have a trait

Through what color glasses does your character see the world? This will help the audience to know both your character and how to play with you. Are you a brown-noser? Do you evaluate everything on a basis of personal gain? Are you most concerned about the comfort of others? Having a clearly defined point of view allows you to have a clear (and anticipatable) response to events.

Get physical

Let your character's body be recognizable. Create an identifiable physical rhythm and posture. That is one of the quickest and easiest means by which an audience can identify and remember a character.

Put words in your mouth

What is your catchphrase? Do you address people in a certain way? What type of exclamation do you use? Is there a particular way that you begin or end statements? Give yourself verbal standards and use them consistently.

Proper is the norm

Proper behavior provides a backdrop against which the unexpected and unconventional can play. However, it often seems to be more difficult for interactors to be proper than improper. There are two reasons for this. The first is the actor's desire to create characters that are unique.

> *I realize that women in this era would never lift their skirts above their knees, but my character is different. She is a free spirit and refuses to be bound by the social restrictions of the period.*

There is nothing wrong with creating unique characters, but if the cast is made up entirely of non-conformists, an unconventional character ceases to be unconventional.

A second reason that actors sometimes won't play proper as the norm is that they impose their own value systems on the time.

It is demeaning for a woman to behave as though it is normal for women to be treated as second-class citizens.

Yes. Yes, yes, yes! And it sets a bad example, too. But if you don't establish that perspective as the norm, there is nothing against which to demonstrate a revolt. Remember that playing a role does not indicate endorsement of that behavior. Playing Oedipus doesn't mean the actor is endorsing patricide, incest, and self-mutilation.

My character is a vagrant. He doesn't care about propriety. He'd sit on the President's desk without thinking twice.

Maybe. Or maybe the actor is taking this opportunity to demonstrate his personal conviction that people shouldn't be intimidated by position.

The third reason that the norm goes by the wayside is that actors get bored, so they introduce new elements. That is not bad if an element fits within the norm of the character in the environment. But sometimes the actor introduces something that is outside the normal realm of her character.

> *Grandma is at Junior's party. Suddenly, Junior calls out, "Dance it, Granny." The actress playing Granny is a great dancer, so she cuts loose, to the amazement of all.*

Did Grandma cut loose because it is part of her character or because the actress playing her wanted to do something a little different for a change?

If you are going to do something that violates the expected norm of your character, make sure your decision is there to serve the narrative, not just to spice things up.

It is also important to bear in mind that if your character breaks the norm, the consequences of your action should be playable. A lack of consequence diminishes the impact of a violation of the norm.

> *"Your Majesty, I will not bow before you. What is more, I spit upon the ground before you."*

Elizabeth should have this insolent peasant beheaded immediately, but Equity has rules about such practices. The best she can do is have her guards rough up the rogue and let him go. The inability to behead diminishes the impact of the defiance.

Being is interesting

Actors are at home on the stage, so it is easy to forget the entertainment value an audience gets out of just being right next to actors who are performing with such consistency and attention to detail that they seem actually to "be" the characters whom they are portraying.

Picture yourself standing on stage next to a celebrity of your choice. Not very stimulating scene work; yet this is the type of experience that is often remembered long after the show is forgotten.

Interactoring
Environment

A character's specific relationship to the environment helps create depth, texture, and context within the narrative. The interactor's awareness of the environment of the play needs to be more premeditated than an improvisor's (because improvisors often are starting from scratch) and more comprehensive than an actor's (because the actor knows in advance the limitations that have already been defined by script and blocking).

Backstories of the immediate environment

A backstory is any type of history that creates a relationship between your character and another character or between your character and an object or a location. Props and sets are lifeless stage dressing until they are colored by backstories.

Traditional theatre allows you the luxury of pre-planning where you will be and what you will come in contact with in the course of a show. Then it's off to the library for a bit of research. Improvisation pulls from the facts you have at your command and your skills as an inventor. Interacting gives you the best of both worlds.

There is an anticipatable environmental structure within which you will be playing, so you can put in your time at the library. What happens within that structure is constantly in flux, so you can flex your inventive muscles as well.

A backstory may be related to a specific object or place.

> *"This is the very knife that my uncle used to teach me to play mumblety-peg."*

Or a backstory may be more generally related to some element of the environment.

> *"My uncle was a drunken butcher, so I've always been squeamish around knives."*

The environment within which you are playing takes on a whole new perspective when you see it through the lens of a character-related backstory.

The purpose of creating backstories is not to have swell anecdotes to tell:

> *"Did I ever tell you about the time my uncle taught me to play mumblety-peg?"*

The value of backstories is that they provide the raw material from which come small details that enrich and color your character's relationship to the environment.

Glancing at the knife, "I wonder what old Uncle Eddie is up to these days."

The small details create the illusion of real life.

Knowledge of the surrounding environment

Interactive work frequently requires that you draw from a knowledge of the world at large in which the story takes place. This surrounding environment is comprised of billions and billions of details. Don't attempt to become an encyclopedia. A performing fact repository is eminently boring. Do what you do best: be an artist. Pick and choose the details that will be most potent and playable within the world that you are creating.

What is playable? Elements that relate to the lives of characters within the show are good. Think in terms of places and things that are part of daily routines. The mundane and day-to-day can be rich in playable possibilities. Think about what details are an important part of your day-to-day life, and then find parallels in the life and world of your character.

You are playing a survivor in a post-apocalyptic society. Brushing your teeth becomes

smearing them with petroleum jelly to prevent
neutron-decay. Going to the market becomes
night raids on neighboring camps. It's a dif-
ferent world, but there are still certain
conventions of everyday life.

A practical working knowledge of the environment at large provides useful reference
points and details that reinforce the illusion of
whatever reality is being played.

Create a common knowledge world

Backstories and environment building are
not new ideas. They have been part of the actor's
toolbox for a long time. But don't get caught
reading some other actor's notebook. In most
states that's a hanging offense. There seems to be
a fear that public knowledge will make the information less potent.

What is unique in the interactor's situation
is that information, when shared as part of a
body of group common knowledge, becomes all
the more potent. When the full cast has a shared
awareness of information that is either environ-
ment-specific or character-specific, that
common knowledge becomes a resource from
which to build rich narrative. Such common
knowledge allows the best of both worlds to exist

simultaneously: the depth of a predetermined focus and the flexibility of an open-ended structure.

Interactoring
Script and Improv

Brilliant on script, dazzling when improvising, but switch back and forth between the two, and a couple of gremlins sometimes pop up. Here they are.

Improv - soft, script - loud

Be careful when switching from improvised lines to lines that have been scripted and rehearsed. Interactors sometimes tend to speak improvised lines softly, and then, when moving into script, suddenly the voice becomes full and commanding. This probably happens because the improvised lines aren't thought of as "real" lines. Remember, the audience doesn't know what has been scripted and what is spontaneous. Don't give them a "volume clue."

Play the subtext — don't speak it

In traditional theatre, actors are always searching for the subtext. In improvisation, there is a tendency to turn subtext into dialogue. In life, people do not always say what is on their minds. But watch what they do, and their feelings and thoughts quickly become clear.

Speak the subtext, and characters appear flat and one-dimensional. Play the subtext as action, and the characters become more interesting and life-like.

It's all real acting

For some reason, improvising is sometimes perceived as a bastard son to "real acting." Treat it as such and that is what it becomes. Let this bias affect an interactive performance and it will destroy the continuity and the magic of the form.

You wouldn't break character when doing Shakespeare. Don't break when you're improvising. Maintain the same discipline, respect, and commitment to your work, whether you are acting, improvising, or interacting.

It's all real acting.

Interactoring
Alone Together

"Let's go someplace where we can be alone together."

Alone together. It's the paradox of inter-active performing.

Interactoring is about connecting—with interactors, with spectactors, with fellow human beings. It is the process of coming together.

But *together* implies a previous state of separation that has been altered. (Or perhaps vice versa.) And so it is that to make a connection, the only thing you can ultimately bring is yourself. Just you. Alone.

There you are: alone together. A paradox, a paradox, a most ingenious paradox.

If you are looking for a solution to the paradox, seek it in other books. Here you will find only a reminder that interactoring alone/together is worth the price of admission.

CONCLUSION

Why do interactive theatre?

It may seem a bit late in the book to ask this question, but here it is. There are all kinds of practical answers: Financial and commercial viability spring to mind; the socio-political and psychological impact of the form cannot be ignored. But perhaps it's just because . . .

The black duvetyne stage drapes had become the dark stone walls in a prison of unspeakable horrors. The dissident, played by an interactor, had been charged with treason and sentenced to death.

The light board operator brought up dimmers 12 through 18 in a morning sunrise, and a spectactor guard shackled the dissident in preparation for his execution. As they turned to leave, a voice called from the dark of the auditorium:

"Wait."

The unexpected audience member rose from her seat and walked up onto the stage.

"I will walk with you."

She allowed herself to be shackled alongside the condemned man. Then, together, the players walked upstage toward a sunrise of endless possibilities.

AFTERWORDS

Appendix

Environmental Interactive

Unlike interactive forms that use theatrical conventions (e.g., using a blue scarf to represent a river, dimming the lights to indicate the passage of time), environmental work assumes the illusion of real life. The story is played out in a location that is used for its "reality value" (e.g., a mansion or a mountain trail) and the story happens in "real time" (i.e., there is no cutting to scenes that take place hours, days, or millennia later). Interactive murder mysteries and Renaissance faires are examples of interactive environmental shows.

In environmental work the audience members are frequently free to wander wherever they choose, whenever they please. Often, the interaction takes place with small groups; therefore, not all of the audience will have access to the same information.

The logistics of the environmental form create unique challenges and opportunities. This appendix suggests some guidelines for environmental interactive performance.

Let them know you are performing

When you are performing in any area that an audience does not recognize as being a stage, it is vital that you make it clear that you are "performing" (even if the performance happens to be "real life" for your character). Many people will not look at an event unless they are sure it is something they are "supposed" to see, for fear of being caught watching.

There are several ways to make clear to an audience that what you are doing is a performance and is meant to be watched.

Make yourself seen

Position yourself so that your audience can easily see you. Find a way to justify standing on any object that will give you height, such as a rock, stump, or table.

Extend your physicality. Expand and stretch your movements and gestures.

Make yourself heard

Project your voice so that people in your general area can hear you easily, even if they are not the people with whom you are speaking. Allow your conversations to be "overheard" by the people who surround you.

Play for truth, not reality

When actors perform a "realistic" play on the stage, they are not behaving realistically. (In real life there is no need to cheat downstage, and no back row that needs to hear what you say.) But doing things that are not natural does not keep traditional actors from creating an illusion of reality.

In environmental theatre, don't let the techniques of "playing big" become an excuse to turn your performance into a cartoon, a parody, or a lampoon. By playing big but truthfully, you can create an illusion of reality in which the audience has the opportunity to observe and relate to a real, living character.

Audience identifiers

Endowing spectators with characters can be challenging in an environmental setting. They often cling to their real life identities and are not ready to play as characters within the show.

Even actors are sometimes hesitant to endow spectactors with identities, for fear that a previous actor may have endowed the spectactor as someone else.

But there is a solution: audience identifiers.

Audience identifiers allow the entire cast to relate to certain spectactors as specific characters, based on some element of the spectactors' physical appearance. (You don't need an identifier for every spectactor in attendance.) Here is an example of a brief audience identifier list.

Short sleeve shirt = Gambler
Long sleeve shirt = Rancher
Boots = Outlaw

The endowments are not fully defined characters as much as they are character categories. The categories become even more playable when they have an obvious relationship to one of the interactor characters; e.g., Hat = Member of Sheriff Cooper's posse

The physical identifiers should never be made obvious to the audience. Audience members should have no idea why it is that every performer they meet seems to know that they are members of Sheriff Cooper's posse.

Wrong: "Ah, I see you are wearing a hat. You must be a member of Sheriff Cooper's posse."

Right: "I heard that Sheriff Cooper couldn't have brought in the Miller gang without your help."

The physical identifiers should be easily visible from far away (e.g., color of eyes is not an as good an identifier as color of hair).

Avoid assigning identifiers that are subject to interpretation (e.g., using "bald men" as an identifying physical trait may simply lead to long and heated discussions about what degree of hair loss constitutes baldness).

Keep the physical traits and endowments as simple as possible.

Avoid designing overlapping identifiers.

Let's see, she's wearing a short-sleeve shirt, boots, and a hat. She must be an outlaw gambler who is masquerading as a member of Sheriff Cooper's posse.

Beware of allowing the identifiers to degenerate into gags.

You: "Howdy. You must be one of Cooper's troopers."

OA: "Super-duper."

Soon there will be a whole posse of spectactors running about, announcing their allegiance to the "Super-Duper Cooper's Troopers Pooper-Scoopers." Spectactors tend to gravitate to the easy joke and short-circuit the potential for developing a story. They don't know any better; you do. Don't encourage gagging.

Real-life vs. Endowment

Take interactive work off the stage and there is a natural tendency toward an awkward duality: You endow spectators and speak to them as characters and they answer you as the person they are in real life.

> *"I'll bet those three kids of yours are just sprouting like weeds."*
>
> *"I don't have any kids."*

You can decrease the odds that the spect-actor will block you by making your offer something that is obviously playing or pretending.

> *"Sorry to hear about your barn burning down."*
>
> *"Yeah, we lost most of the cattle."*

If you can't do it, don't pursue it

In environmental, you are bound by the reality of what can *truly* happen. In other styles (e.g., Theatrical Freestyle) you have the freedom to create almost any possibility through the use of theatrical conventions, metaphor, and artistic license. But in environmental work, everything must appear to be real.

When you are pursuing action in an environmental setting, be sure the action has the potential to really happen; otherwise, you will wind up *cul-de-sacking* to get yourself out of the situation.

> *"We can pan for gold until we've got enough to bail Bart of of jail."*

This is great interactive action as long as there really is a place to pan for gold. If there is not, it's only a clever idea that won't pan out to anything.

Environmental hand-offs

Because the audience is free to move throughout the entire environment, hand-offs take on new possibilities.

As you finish an interaction with a spectactor, create a reason for the spectactor to seek out another character, by linking that character to an offer that the spectactor has made. Many people enjoy the thrill of the hunt, seeking out other characters who relate to their story.

"Sorry to hear you lost your cattle. You should talk to Sheriff Cooper, I hear tell he's got a few head he's lookin' to sell."

For an environmental hand-off to work effectively, you need to give spectactors an easy way to locate and recognize the character they are seeking and a clear understanding of what they should do when they find the character.

You could probably find Sheriff Cooper down at the Silver Slipper Saloon. He usually drops by there around three every afternoon. You know what he looks like, don't you? He's a tall fellow. Wears a white hat. And he has that big old silver star on his vest. When you see him, tell him you're interested in buying some of his cattle."

Character

Environmental work frequently does not allow much time "backstage" to take a break from the performance. When developing your character for an environmental production, remember that your physical and emotional choices will have to be sustained over extended periods of time. A hunch-backed misanthrope with one lame leg may be great character choice, but it will start to take its toll when played for extended periods of time.

Eavesdropping

In environmental settings there is often so much happening at once that a spectactor cannot possibly be aware of it all. This creates a golden opportunity to apply a magical technique of environmental interactive—eavesdropping.

To eavesdrop, find a place in which, without being observed, you can listen in on an interaction between a spectactor and an actor. Mentally note the offers that are initiated by the spectactor. When the interchange is over, tail the spectactor for a while, staying out of sight until a little time has passed. Then approach the spectactor and start interacting, making an overt offer that ties in with the spectactor's offer that you overheard.

> *You have overheard a spectactor say that she shot and killed the infamous outlaw Six-gun Sam. Later on, she finds you seated next to her at the bar at the Silver Slipper Saloon, drowning your sorrows in bad whiskey. You invite her to share a drink, and she eventually learns that you are mourning the loss of your bosom*

buddy, whose name just happens to be Six-gun Sam.

Give and Take

Because focus can be very scattered in environmental interactive, it is especially important to be aware when a fellow actor is trying to command the focus of everyone present. When this happens, it is imperative that all other actors give focus immediately. Without such courtesy, everyone's work will suffer from the resulting confusion.

The price and the reward

Environmental interactive is difficult, because it never acknowledges its own unreality. It requires you to overcome all the hurdles of interactive work without the benefit of being able to step outside the premise.

It takes total commitment, incredible ingenuity, and great stamina. The demands of environmental interactive are enormous. But when it is successful, so are the rewards.

Related Reading

<u>Acts of Service: Spontaneity, Commitment,</u>
<u>Tradition in the Nonscripted Theatre</u>
Jonathan Fox
To be released in 1994

Drawing on the author's background in oral studies and experimental theatre, this book will address the history, nature, and role of nonscripted theatre in effecting social transformation. A major section will focus on specific procedures for the production of nonscripted performances from the perspective of Playback Theatre.

<u>*Commedia dell'Arte:* An Actor's Handbook</u>
John Rudlin
Routledge, 1994

A guide to using *commedia* techniques in performance. Includes a section that details the basis for improvising each of the stock characters from the *commedia* and a section that covers some of the applications of *commedia* in twentieth-century theatre.

<u>Games for Actors and Non-Actors</u>
Augusto Boal
Routledge, 1992

A book of exercises to build the skills and sensitivities to do the varied forms of Theatre of the Oppressed. Also includes detailed definitions, explanations, and examples of the T.O. interactive theatre forms.

Impro: Improvisation and the Theatre
Keith Johnstone
Theatre Arts Books, 1979

Presented in the form of practical experiences, this book contains a wealth of concepts and techniques that enhance the quality of improvisational work. Each of the sections—Status, Spontaneity, Narrative Skills, and Masks and Trance—is rich with examples that bring the techniques to life.

Improvisation
John Hodgson & Ernest Richards
Methuen, 1966

Discusses the value and applications of improvisation, as well as presenting methods and exercises. Includes sections on the use of improvisation to develop a traditional script and expanding the depth and texture of a scripted show though the use of improvisation.

Improvisation for the Theatre
Viola Spolin
Northwestern University Press, 1963

A vast reference work that focuses on freeing the natural ability to play and perform through the use of improvisational theatre games. Also includes sections on coaching improvisation and working with children.

Improvisation Through Theatre Sports
Lynda Belt & Rebecca Stockley
Thespis Productions, 1989

Presented in curriculum form appropriate for class instruction, the book presents a logical progression of exercises for building acting and improvisational skills. Includes many concepts and exercises from Keith Johnstone's work and provides a model for producing a Theatre Sports competition.

Improvising Real Life: Personal Story in Playback Theatre
Jo Salas
Kendall/Hunt Publishing, 1993

Presents the history, techniques, and principles of the interactive form, Playback Theatre, developed by Jonathan Fox, in which stories told by the audience are "played back" by improvisational performers. Includes chapters on ritual, use of music, and conducting.

Playing Boal: Theatre, Therapy, Activism
ed. Mady Schutzman & Jan Cohen-Cruz
Routledge, 1994

A collection of essays by practitioners of Theatre of the Oppressed, in which the strengths and weaknesses of T.O. in different cultural contexts are addressed, as well as focusing on the ways in which T.O. forms have been modified to make them more effective in different settings..

Scenarios of the *Commedia dell'Arte*
Trans. & ed. Henry F. Salerno
Limelight Editions

A collection of fifty complete plots from the *commedia dell'arte,* presented in scenario form. This book can be used as a model for understanding scenario-driven, rather than script-driven, performances.

Theatre of the Oppressed
Augusto Boal
Urizen Books, 1979

Essays on the hazards of traditional theatre as a form of oppression, and the history and techniques of interactive theatre forms developed by Boal to combat oppression, including Forum Theatre, Image Theatre, and Invisible Theatre.

Tony n' Tina's Wedding
Artificial Intelligence, conceived by Nancy Cassaro
Samuel French, Inc., 1994

A full-scale script for an environmental interactive show. The book includes multi-page character outlines; a timeline with scenes in script and scenario form; and production notes, including specific advice on how to conduct auditions and rehearsals geared to meet the specific needs of environmental interactive theatre. Comprehensive in scope, the book also includes sections on props, costumes, food, floor plans, and trouble-shooting.

<u>Truth in Comedy: The Manual of Improvisation</u>
Charna Halpern, Del Close, Kim Johnson
Meriwether Publishing Ltd., 1994

A book presenting the structure and techniques for performing "Harolds," long-form improvisations, in which full-length shows are created around central themes through improvisation.

Glossary

The terms in this glossary come from a variety of sources; some have definitions other that those you will find here. The purpose of including these definitions is not to appropriate the words, but rather to clarify their meanings as applied to the concepts of interactive theatre found within this book. [Brackets indicate page references.]

accept: to respond to an offer in a way that affirms the truth and fulfills the intent of the offer. [46]

anachronism: any offer that violates the reality of the established premise. [145]

assumption: See *endow.*

audience identifiers: a system by which cast members can relate to certain spectactors as specific characters, based on some element of the spectactors' physical appearance. Used in environmental interactive. [191]

backlead: to free (encourage) spectactors to contribute to the narrative on their own initiative through techniques that increase spectactor confidence

by creating opportunities for success in performance. [103]

backstory: any type of history that creates a
relationship between your character and an object, location, or other character. [176]

bend: to accept and redirect an offer through justification. [134]

blank slate: improvising without any predetermined information. The C.R.O.W. is developed
from ideas that occur while improvising. [51]

blind offer: an offer that is made unconsciously,
without conscious intent to communicate information. [40]

block: to undermine the truth or intent of an
offer. [43]

B.M.E.T.: beginning, middle, end, tag; a structure
for creating narrative. [64]

build: an offer that supports and expands a previous offer by accepting and adding new
information. [47]

character breaker: an offer made for the sole purpose of forcing a player to behave in a way that
violates his character. [77]

connect the dots: a backlead in which the spect-actor is presented with two independent but related pieces of information, allowing the spect-actor to make the connection. [124]

conflict loop: trouble that doesn't lead to resolution or evolution. [83]

covert cueing: cueing a spectactor in such a way that the audience is unaware of the cueing. [105]

C.R.O.W.: character, relationship, objective, and where; the essential elements upon which an improvisational scene or story is built. [53]

cue: to facilitate spectactor participation by giving the spectactor instructions of what to do. [104] (Also, see *overt cueing* and *covert cueing.*)

cul-de-sac: to pursue action that leads you back to exactly the same place you began, with no further progress in the story. [81]

deny, denial: See *block*

endow: to relate to a person, object, location, or situation as though it possessed specific qualities or attributes. [41, 109]

environmental interactive: an interactive form that assumes the illusion of "real life." The story is performed in a location that is used for its "reality value," and the story happens in "real time." [6, 189]

fill in the blank: a backlead in which the inter-actor pauses in mid-sentence, allowing the spectactor to fill in the gap with an offer. [123]

gag: to go for a laugh at the expense of the narra-tive or character. [45]

give and take: the process by which performers pass information and focus to one another. [48, 198]

hand-off: giving a spectactor a reason to seek out and interact with another character. [139, 195]

hook: a spectactor's offer, or a possession, skill, or attribute belonging to a spectactor, that is later reincorporated into a pay-off. [139]

improvisation: the creation of a story through unscripted performance. Done by improvisors (who know the guidelines of improvisation), not by spectactors (who don't). [37]

intentional offer: an offer made with the con-scious intent of communicating specific information. [40]

interacting: interactors and spectactors collaborating in the creation of a performance. [87, 165]

Interactive Theatre: any theatrical form in which the audience takes a proactive role, participating as a collaborator with the performers in the creation of the show. [1]

interactor: a member of the cast (not the audience) who performs in an interactive show. [87, 165]

justify: to generate a reason that makes it clear why an offer supports the premise. [71, 134]

lead and fill: a method of improvising in which all major narrative devlopments are initiated by one performer (lead) and supported by all the other performers (fill). [166]

link: to tie an unrelated story element into the existing narrative. [58]

monkeywrench: to introduce "trouble" into the narrative, then sit back, do nothing, and watch others try to deal with the consequences. [76]

multiple choice: a backlead in which the spectactor is given a variety of options from which to choose an offer. [122]

nail: to make an offer for the purpose of getting another performer, rather than his or her character, in trouble. [77]

narrative: the story. [51]

neg, negate: See *block.*

OA (obnoxious audience): audience members whose participation becomes such a disruption to an interactive performance that it ruins the show for the rest of the audience. [156]

offer: anything that a person says or does. [40] (See also *blind offer* and *intentional offer.)*

overt cueing: to cue a spectactor in such a way that the audience is aware of the cue. [105]

pay-off: the resolution of a scene through the reincorporation of a hook. [139]

peg: any story element within the narrative. [55]

peel the onion: revealing contradictory traits within a character as a source of good trouble. [72]

periphery: story elements that are related to a central theme or topic. [55]

premise: the assumed period, location, characters, and plot upon which an improvisational or interactive performance is based. [145]

primers: backleading formats that make it quicker and easier for a spectactor to play. [120]

reincorporation: linking an element brought up earlier in the narrative to the current situation. [61]

routine: any type of action or event that, if it goes according to plan, will be relatively predictable; also, the way in which the action is usually done. [81]

sidetracking: going off on a narrative tangent and failing to pursue or resolve an established narrative direction. [80]

spectactor: an audience member who becomes a performer within an interactive show. [37, 99, 152, 155]

step: an increment of "room" provided by an interactor so that a spectactor may fill it with his or her own offer. [117]

stroke: to give positive reinforcement to a spectactor for his or her offer. [130]

tag: a brief ending handle that helps the audience reflect on the story or scene they have just seen. [64. 68]

talking heads: a scene which is all talking and no doing. [80]

trouble: the element that is resolved or evolved to create a satisfying story. [70]

weave: to integrate spectactors and their offers into the existing plot in such a way that both become essential to the story. [138]

wimp: to make a vague, undefined offer. [41]

wirth: Jeff's last name.

About the author

Jeff Wirth is nationally recognized as a leading proponent of interactive theatre in the United States. He has served as editor of the Interactive Theatre Newsletter since 1992 and has been involved in the development of interactive theatre since 1978. His credentials include Artistic Director for Circle Theatre, Producing Director of the Performance Corps, and Director of Interactive Performance for the Pennsylvania Renaissance Faire. Mr. Wirth has also served on the Fullerton College drama faculty, teaching classes in movement, improvisation, and interactive theatre.

As part of his personal mission to establish interactive theatre as a popular and recognized form, Mr. Wirth is working to create interactive training programs at colleges, universities, and conservatories nationwide.

Stay up-to
on the lat
in the field of interactive theatre—